# Keeping Customers *and* Getting Their Friends Too!

**Dorothy M. Tuma**

Illustrated by Stanislaus Olonde "Stano"

Keeping Customers
and Getting Their Friends Too!
Copyright © 2017 Dorothy M. Tuma
The moral right of the author has been asserted.
All rights reserved. No part of this publication may be reproduced, stored in a retrieval system, or transmitted, in any form or by any means, without prior permission in writing of the author, nor be otherwise circulated in any form other than that in which it is published.
First published 2011.
Editor: Aryantungyisa K. Otiti
Design and Typesetting: Jazzy Designs Ltd Illustrations: Stanislaus Olonde "Stano"

ISBN-13: 9781977578730
ISBN-10: 197757873X

# Disclaimer

This publication is designed to provide competent and reliable information regarding the subject matter covered. The author and publisher specifically disclaim any liability that may be incurred from the use or application of the contents of this book.

*To my parents, Ruth and Tom*
*For always pushing us to do our best*

# Keeping Customers and Getting Their Friends Too!

A great book that addresses a matter that is fundamental to excellence in service provision. The principles in here are universal and timeless.

**Dennis Kawuma, Business Editor**
**Daily Monitor Newspaper**
**Kampala, Uganda.**

Well written, very fine identifiable examples, a true gem. There are so many morsels of expert advice that it will be a crime not to have it as one of the manuals for any company that cherishes their customers. The book is different because it doesn't pontificate...a lot of things stated and put across elect an "Oh, yeah, I know that, and can do that!" My staff will read it as a MUST, and will be measured against it.

**Geoffrey T. Kihuguru, Chief Executive Officer**
**Pentad Insurance Services Ltd.**
**Kampala, Uganda.**

Refreshing, engaging, insightful and practical. Regional integration means increased competition and only the competitive businesses will survive. This indigenously grown and well written book shows you just how you can include customer retention as part of your success formula.

**Agatha Nderitu, Executive Director 2010 - 2012**
**East African Business Council**
**Arusha, Tanzania.**

This book is the first of its kind on customer care – written in the African context based on customer care experiences by African businesses. The book is a simple-to-read handbook on maximising the customer care experience and is a must-have for business people, entrepreneurs as well as trainers and educators in customer care. It is a rare resource with potential to transform customer care practice and attitudes among our business practitioners. The numerous cases imbibe the book with such useful illustrations and are carefully documented with such dexterity to change your attitude towards customer care and equip you with the necessary tools on how to do it, improve it and keep your customers.

The principles contained in this book are not only insightful to the reader but are carefully illustrated to ensure immediate grasp, relate the subject with one's unique situation and to ensure that no single reader fails to benefit. The book is written in a flowing conversational style with language that guarantees both the starters and those familiar with the subject immense benefit. I recommend the book to all practicing business people, customer care professionals, educators in business schools, trainers and business consultants and all those who care about business transformation in Africa.

**Geoffrey Bakunda, PhD, Associate Professor and**
**Dean Faculty of Marketing and Hospitality Management**
**Makerere University Business School**
**Kampala, Uganda.**

## TABLE OF CONTENTS

|  | Foreword | XIII |
|---|---|---|
|  | Acknowledgments | XV |
|  | Introduction | XVII |
| Chapter 1 | A Place to Begin | 1 |
| Chapter 2 | Make Positive First Impressions | 10 |
| Chapter 3 | Be Courteous | 24 |
| Chapter 4 | Practice Honesty | 40 |
| Chapter 5 | Just Do Your Job | 57 |
| Chapter 6 | Deliver With Speed | 74 |
| Chapter 7 | Communicate | 88 |
| Chapter 8 | Offer Seamless Service | 103 |
| Chapter 9 | Go the Extra Mile | 121 |

Chapter 10  Value Feedback · · · · · · · · · · · · · · · · · · · · · · · · · · · · · 138

Chapter 11  Compensate For Errors· · · · · · · · · · · · · · · · · · · · · · · · 154

Chapter 12  Demonstrate Appreciation · · · · · · · · · · · · · · · · · · · · 168

Chapter 13  Equip and Reward Your Staff · · · · · · · · · · · · · · · · · · 180

Chapter 14  Monitor the Competition · · · · · · · · · · · · · · · · · · · · · 190

Chapter 15  Put It into Practice · · · · · · · · · · · · · · · · · · · · · · · · · · 196

End Notes · · · · · · · · · · · · · · · · · · · · · · · · · · · · · · · · 199

# Foreword

The impact of customer retention in the market place cannot be undervalued. With a limited market from which to source customers, you must cultivate and coax customer loyalty to bear the fruit of customer advocacy for your product.

Successful customer retention starts with the first contact an organization has with a customer and continues throughout the entire lifetime of the relationship. A company's ability to attract and retain new customers, is not only related to its product or services, but strongly related to the way it services its existing customers and the reputation it creates within and across the marketplace.

In "Keeping Customers – And getting their friends too!" Dorothy Tuma brings to light the attitudes of service providers, while presenting the often ignored and misinterpreted perspective of the customer. This book is an excellent insight into what really goes on with service providers primarily in East Africa and every reader will identify with most of the real life stories and experiences shared. The tact, wit and insight with which they are narrated opens one's eyes to the deeper nuances missed in interpretation and consequently helps give the service provider a perspective on the customer's experience and decision making process thereafter.

One of the unique factors in this book is the practical do-it-yourself exercises that are not only apt, but also elevate this book from an ordinary business skills book to a life changing business manual on customer retention practices that actually work.

In her book, Dorothy Tuma shows that customer retention is more than just giving customers what they expect; it is about anticipating and exceeding customer expectations and thus turning them into loyal advocates for your brand. "Keeping Customers" shows us the gaps in our market that need to be filled to achieve this. The key differentiator in a competitive environment is more often than not the delivery of a consistently high standard of customer service as demonstrated by various companies quoted in this book. Needless to say the results speak for themselves.

Customer retention has a direct impact on profitability and not only does it reduce the need for marketing and advertising, as illustrated by the author, it assists in needs assessment because a satisfied customer will more or less always voice their opinion on how you can improve your service. This comes from the confidence they have that you actually care about their thoughts on what you offer and this trust can only be built by your continuous display of an interest not only in profiting from them but also in caring about their wellbeing and satisfaction with your product.

In this competitive business environment, if you care about keeping your customers and getting their friends too, this book is exactly what you need. It is an excellent start on your journey towards achieving this goal. I urge you and your staff to engage in the practical exercises the author has so creatively spelled out; we at National Water and Sewerage Corporation shall certainly try them. Your business will reap the benefits. And when you are through, be sure to recommend this valuable handbook to your friends. "Keeping Customers - And getting their friends too!" is a fresh and inspiring look at customer service, a much needed and timely tool to help you improve your business.

**Professor Dr. William T. Muhairwe,**
**Managing Director 1998 - 2011**
**National Water and Sewerage Corporation**
**Kampala, Uganda.**

# Acknowledgments

I am indebted to Monitor Publications Ltd., for all the support editorial and promotional. To the Monitor Business Desk for recognizing the potential in what was just an idea for a column and giving me a platform on which to compliment great service, point out poor service and suggest remedies. The pieces I had to submit every week for Dora's Diary are the very core of this book. Thank you for the opportunity.

I owe a debt of gratitude to everyone who contributed stories of good and poor customer service to Dora's Diary. To my closest circle of friends and regular contributors: Jackie, Judy, Sarah, Selina and Stella; to my family and all my contributing readers – thank you!

To all the loyal readers of Dora's Diary, especially those who e-mail feedback – thank you for showing me that the column indeed adds value to your professional lives. You gave me the idea of turning the column into a book.

Professor Dr. William T Muhairwe, for finding time in your busy schedule to review the manuscript and write the Foreword for this book.

David Sseppuuya, for an Introduction that sets the perfect tone for the reader.

Thank you to all the book's reviewers; Dennis Kawuma, Geoffrey Kihuguru, Agatha Nderitu and Dr. Geoffrey Bakunda. I appreciate your having sacrificed the time to recommend the book and offer your invaluable opinions and advice.

To my entire family – thank you for all the story submissions, encouragement and moral support. In addition to that, I thank my brother Zik for all the legal tips, critical reviews and ideas on taking this book beyond just the newspaper articles.

Dad - for making the first words you said to me every time we talked for the year preceding this book's publication – "How far with the book?" Such pressure! It is a relief not to have to answer that question anymore - Thanks for the push!

"Stano" my illustrator – thank you for your amazing illustrations which truly speak a thousand words.

Aryantu, my editor – for your patience; and for getting the manuscript to read more like an engaging book than a weekly newspaper column! For all your suggestions on how we might truly deliver value – thank you!

# INTRODUCTION

We have all been to the market, to the bank, to the hospital, to the border control. Put another way, we have all worked in the market, in the bank, in the hospital, at the border control, or any number of places and institutions. What are our experiences in relating to others, be they external people or colleagues from within? My own experience in countries like Uganda is unforgettable – not for the exemplary way I have been handled, but rather for the ill-manner. I have also occasionally been caught on the wrong side of treating others. Indeed the institutions I have been a part of have often been wanting in their care.

These experiences make one wonder why a person is in the job; why the institution exists at all. If it is a service company, why does it behave like the military? Even the military is shaped on discipline. If the person is a receptionist, why do they not receive, other than repel? If the role is to communicate, why not put across the appropriate information, in the right time, and with the commensurate attitude? If it is treating the wounded, why add insult to injury? If it is to build bridges, why break them in the first instance?

As Uganda's economy grows, so too does the service sector. But service sector growth should not be limited to mere numbers and size. The width must be complimented by depth, however as most business owners know, this does not always come automatically. It is an attitude, a skill that must be consciously developed in our service sector. Through this book -"Keeping Customers - And getting their friends too!" Dorothy

Tuma meets this need. The author takes the reader through a typical business encounter and with vivid examples from real life, she points out the essence of customer service, its sheer necessity, and the fact that a little more attention to detail and a little more care for the other person can be the difference between a successful enterprise and a struggling one.

Along with these interesting examples, the author gives practical tips and exercises that will help both business owners and service providers to sharpen their skills. Consequently they will improve and grow their businesses. The book is an interesting read and also a pleasure to apply. I urge you to make use of this book; you will harvest the full benefit for your business.

**David Sseppuuya,**
**Executive Editor 2010 - 2012**
**Monitor Publications Ltd.**
**Kampala, Uganda.**

# CHAPTER 1
# A Place To Begin

You are in business to make the largest profit you possibly can[i]. Profits however, are simply what is left over from the revenue your customers bring to you, less all the financial obligations your business must meet. If you agree with this definition, you will also agree that customers are the very life blood of your business. If you are running a legitimate business, without customers you will soon either have to close your doors for good or sell your business to someone who believes they will be better at attracting and retaining customers. It follows therefore, that every existing business remains operational because it has customers who believe the business in question provides a product or service that fulfils one or more of their wants, needs or both. That puts customers in an incredibly strong position.

In the countries where businesses face strong competition, customers reign supreme. Businesses do everything they can to attract and retain customers. Sophisticated business enterprises spend the equivalent of millions of dollars every year on attempting to establish relationships with customers and getting to understand their preferences in order to tailor products and services to exceed customer expectations.

In our part of the world however, it would appear that the power in the provider/customer relationship still lies primarily in the hands of the provider. In other words, instead of courting customers and making them feel special at every turn, most providers make their customers feel like they are doing them a favour they do not deserve.

With globalization, regional integration, increasing competition and ever more savvy customers however, it is only a matter of time before the pendulum swings, placing the balance of power squarely in customers' hands. The businesses in our part of the world that will succeed when that time comes are the businesses that voluntarily decide to treasure their customers today.

**Some interesting customer retention data[ii]**

- Acquiring new customers can cost five times more than satisfying and retaining current customers

- A 2 percent increase in customer retention has the same effect on profits as cutting costs by 10 percent

- The average company loses 10 percent of its customers each year.

- A 5 percent reduction in a customer defection rate can increase profits by 25 to 125 percent, depending on the industry.

- The customer profitability rate tends to increase over the life of a retained customer.

Research data[iii] shows that it will cost you five times as much to market a product to a new customer than it will to market the same product to an existing customer. The data also shows that on an annual basis, an existing customer is worth at least three times the value of someone who buys a product or service from you just once. Does it not make sense therefore, to retain your existing customers, once you attract them into your fold?

## Know your customer

Who then is your customer? Is it every single person out there? The answer is a resounding "No!" It is important for you to know exactly who your customers are in order for you to avoid spending unnecessary resources pursuing individuals who will never spend any money on what you have to offer. That does not mean that you should ignore the person who walks into your clothing boutique for instance, just because the individual is dressed in a fashion that announces to you that they cannot afford even the cheapest item of clothing you have on display. You need to treat everyone who enters your establishment with respect. On top of the minimum service levels extended to everyone however, you ought to find ways of giving your actual target market, and within your target market, your most loyal customers, a little more than everyone else.

If you do not already have a definition of your target market, spend some time developing one. Beyond identifying your target, you will also need to divide your target market into subgroups commonly referred to as segments, in order to better understand how each sub-group relates to your products or services.

Since defining your target market and segmenting it are not the main subject of this book, we will limit ourselves to a general description of the two terms. Your target market is a specific and narrowly defined group of people that you view as your primary customers. A neighbourhood bakery for instance, could define its target market as young and upcoming professionals, both male and female, who enjoy freshly baked goods but do not have the time to make them. The bakery would then spend its resources on attracting and retaining customers who fit that profile to its doorstep. Who is your target?

Segmenting your market simply refers to dividing your target market into groups or clusters that behave the same way and therefore, may be treated the same way, as a group. Segments usually fall along geographical, demographic, or even behavioural lines. For instance, in the bakery example, the business owner could segment their defined target market along the following lines - the health conscious (only interested in low sugar, low fat options), the sweet tooth (will buy anything sweet) or the daily visitor (goes to the bakery every single day) and the weekend binger (shops only once a week but shops in bulk). See if you can identify behavioural patterns among your customers and use that to help guide you in defining your segments - smaller groups or clusters within your already defined larger group. Can you cluster your customers by the reasons why they buy your products or services, the results they expect from your products or services, the occasions when they buy your products or services or even how often and in what quantities they buy your products or services?

Knowing your target is important because it will save you the unexpected expense of pursuing someone who will never be interested in your products at all. Knowing your segments will allow you to create a customized and meaningful approach for each one. Consider the bottled water manufacturers who offer a variety of packaging types and sizes - five litre dispenser bottles, one litre bottles, 1/2 litre bottles with retractable caps and in some places, 250 millilitre sachets all with a particular target in mind.

Just in case you do not work for a private company and think that this book is not for you because you actually do not have any customers, think again. Broadly speaking, anyone who pays you for the services you offer is your customer. Without them, your entity would cease to exist. The table below shows a few non-businesses that have customers.

Table I: Examples of non-businesses that have customers

| Employer | Customer |
| --- | --- |
| Government Ministry | Tax payers |
| Police Force | Tax payers |
| Hospital | Patients |
| Member Association | Paying members |

## Know what you offer

In addition to knowing your customer, you should know exactly what you have to offer to customers. Why should they come to you instead of to anyone else? The Kampala Serena will tell you that it actually does not have any competitors. Why? Because for their target market, the Serena is the only hotel in town that provides what the Serena has to offer in the manner that the Serena offers it. Customers go to the Serena for the elegant and sophisticated surroundings, decorated in an African motif, the efficient service, and the delicious cuisine all at prices that target a more affluent individual. In both Kampala and Kigali, Khana Khazana an Indian restaurant, has a reputation for excellent dishes. Every single item on the menu has incredible palate appeal. People go to Khana Khazana when they want a guaranteed good meal. McDonald's and Starbucks promise a consistent product no matter where you order it. Their customers have come to expect just that.

Such consistent delivery of a company's offer is not accidental. An extraordinary amount of work goes into defining the offer and its method of delivery. Each staff member knows exactly what their role is in ensuring consistent service or product delivery. The offer is clearly defined, documented and communicated. So are staff roles and customer expectations. Why do people choose you? What is your unique offer to the customer? What sets you apart? For the record, "Location" is not the right answer. Respond from your customer's point of view. A customer would use expressions like "Ease of access" or "Convenience" as opposed to "Location." Ask yourself again, why do customers come to you?

If you own a micro, small or medium size enterprise and think it is impossible for you to differentiate yourself, think again. You too can become the sole supplier[iv] of what you have to offer. In the simplest of terms, in a market where all the tomato sellers sell tomatoes at the same price, you could stand out - and even justify charging a little more which customers would be happy to pay - by being the most polite tomato seller, the only tomato seller who offers complimentary packaging, the only tomato seller who offers complementary onions with purchase or the tomato seller who always has someone on hand to help carry customer groceries to their cars. How will you make your offer stand out?

## Follow your customer's path

Once you are sure of what you have to offer as well as who your customer is, take a walk along your customer's path. List all the steps your customer goes through in order to interact with your product or service. From the point that a customer even thinks of coming to you, what steps do they go through? As you list each step identify what could go wrong at that step (point of pain) and what could go right, or even better than expected (point of pleasure). As a business owner or manager, you will want to enhance the points of pleasure and eliminate the points of pain.

To illustrate, when I think of having dinner at a local restaurant, the first thing I will do is call to make reservations. That telephone call will be a point of pleasure if my call is picked up immediately and a pleasant, polite voice on the other side greets me and asks how they can be of assistance. Such a warm reception already begins to set the tone for the meal that I am making a reservation for.

That call however could also turn out to be a point of pain if I have to wait for several minutes before my call is answered, if the voice that

### Table II: Possible customer path – bookshop

| Step | Potential Point of Pain | Potential Point of Pleasure |
|---|---|---|
| **Situation: Someone recommends a book to a friend.** | | |
| 1. Customer rushes to the bookshop during short lunch break. | Finds bookshop closed, with a sign on the door reading "Back in 15 minutes." | An attendant meets customer at the door with a smile and asks if they can help her find anything. |
| 2. Customer gets to the bookshop and looks for the book but cannot find it. | Sections are not clearly labelled. Customer cannot find the book she is looking for. | Attendants are walking around making sure they give customers any assistance they need. Book sections are clearly labelled. |
| 3. Customer tries to find an attendant to help. | Attendants are nowhere to be found. Attendants are "busy" reading the newspaper or talking on their mobile phones. | Smiling attendants are easy to identify because they are wearing uniforms and are paying attention to customers. |
| 4. Attendant informs customer that they have the book in stock. | Attendant only provides information and then carries on with what they were doing before. | Attendant happily walks customer to the right section of the bookshop, picks out the book and asks if they can offer any other assistance. |
| 5. Customer stands in the check-out line for 20 minutes. | The slow, grumpy looking cashier at the till does not even acknowledge the customer with a greeting. | Additional check-out lanes are opened so lines are shorter and move faster. Smiling cashiers apologize for the delay. |
| 6. The cashier rings up the book. | The book costs more than the advertised price on shelf. The cashier cannot explain the variance in price. Customer storms out without the book. | Cashier's price matches the price on shelf. Cashier quickly serves the customer, thanks them and wishes them a pleasant day. |

responds on the other side is rude and possibly uninformed and if the person on the other side and I are not able to communicate properly with each other, for whatever reason. Any of those points of pain could actually cost you a lost sale because I will simply choose to take my business somewhere else.

Go through the exercise of listing everything your customers do when engaging with your product or service, from beginning to end. Even the last step of the process counts. How have you caused customers pain and what will you do to eliminate it going forward? And how have you caused them pleasure? What will you do to enhance it?

Go through this process for each of the products or services you offer and identify ways to improve your customer's experience with you. Your goal should be to enhance pleasure and eliminate pain.

Finally if you have not yet done this, call your company from an unidentified number and find out exactly how your staff handles customer calls. Send an e-mail to that e-mail address you advertise and see how long it takes to get a response, if ever. If you do get a response, how helpful is it? Would you be pleased with the way your company employees treated you when you proactively attempted to interact with them? If your company has several locations, visit a location where the staff do not know who you are and simply be a customer. Do you like the way you are treated? If yes, how will you make sure that level of service gets duplicated? If not, what needs to change and how?

Now that you have had an opportunity to think about what your customers go through, it is time to take a look at the mistakes and successes of other businesses. Each mini case study is an actual event that happened primarily in Uganda. None of the cases are fabricated; and each teaches a principle of customer service, which serves as the case title. The cases are organized to reflect the different stages a customer goes through from the minute they enter the door to the time they leave, as well as afterwards. As you read each case, think about how you would have handled the same situation. Would you have scored better, worse, just as well or just as poorly as the individuals involved?

To guide your self-assessment, at the end of each chapter you will find a check-list of the principles covered in that particular chapter. The check-list is designed to help you see how well you are doing on each principle discussed. If the principle is one that you currently practice, put a tick in the Yes column. If the principle is one you need to work on, put a tick in the No column. Once you complete the entire check-list, the areas you need to work on if you are to keep your customers and get their friends too, will be very clear.

Some names have been changed to protect the individuals' privacy and company names have been omitted in the majority of the case studies.

## How Are You Doing?
If a principle is one that you currently practice, put a tick (√) in the Yes column. If a principle is one you need to work on, put a tick in the No column.

| A Place to Begin | Yes | No |
|---|---|---|
| Know your customer | | |
| Know what you offer | | |
| Follow your customer's path | | |

# CHAPTER 2
## MAKE POSITIVE FIRST IMPRESSIONS

First impressions really do matter and they really do last. Image experts tell us you only get one chance to make a first impression and that window of opportunity closes in just a few seconds. In the same way, the first few minutes a customer spends in your business premises - or in this electronic age, on your website - are plenty to decide whether they like the place or not and if they have a choice, whether or not they will return. Ensure that your business premises, wherever they are, your staff and service make a strong enough positive impression that stays with customers and keeps them coming back.

Remember how uncomfortable you felt when you went to visit a friend or relative in their home and the people who welcomed you into the house made you feel like a burden they really did not want to bear? In the same way, when customers walk into your premises and are met with the indifferent and sometimes even hostile stares of your employees, all the customers want to do at that point is leave with the money they had planned to spend. Just like you enjoy receiving a warm welcome when you go to a friend's house, your customers enjoy receiving a warm welcome when they choose to enter your premises.

This warm welcome in the form of a smile, a pleasant greeting and an offer to help the customer with whatever they need, is only the beginning. Front line staff should be fully attentive throughout the customer's visit and should be sure to thank the customer for coming in and to wish them a good rest of the day, irrespective of the customer's appearance and irrespective of whether the customer spends money or not.

If you have a website, it should be easy for customers to navigate. The different web pages should be clearly labelled and should not take too long to load as this will cause your more impatient online visitors to simply leave the website without getting what they came for. Just like it should be easy for customers in a brick and mortar establishment to get help when they need it, your online visitors should have easy access to a "Help" page as well as your contact information including e-mail addresses, telephone numbers, your physical and mailing addresses.

In addition to taking note of the welcome and attention they receive, your customers will be taking a good look at both the appearance of your staff and the appearance of the surroundings they find themselves in as they unconsciously categorize your business. How clean are your waiters' uniforms and are they in a state of good repair? Do your employees look upbeat and happy to be at work or are they slouching around, giving the impression that they were forced to be at work that day? Are there groups of employees standing around gossiping because they clearly have nothing better to do? All this is taken note of in a matter of minutes, when a customer first walks in the door.

What impressions do your surroundings give? Does the environment actually support the image you keep on trying to portray? Is the place clean and tidy? Do you leave rubbish strewn all over the floor? Do you have wastepaper baskets and if you do, are they overflowing? Are your toilet facilities clean or are they a health hazard? Having clean toilets is a must for everyone but you should take special care to ensure these facilities are especially clean if you serve food on your premises. Why? Because we all know that the individuals engaged in food preparation and serving use the same facilities the customers do. If those facilities are dirty, chances are high that your food preparers and servers will carry all kinds of bacteria from the dirty toilets back to the kitchen, resulting in upset stomachs for your customers. Customers take note of all these things and if they are not impressed by the way you handle them, they simply will not return. Ensuring that your premises are always presentable should be a clearly designated responsibility. Assign a member of your team to inspect the premises at regular intervals throughout the day.

## Exude a warm welcome

One Sunday a friend and I arrived at a local casino just before 1:00pm, eager to confirm or disprove the rave reviews we kept on hearing about the restaurant there. The gate was closed and the place looked deserted. When the gateman opened the gate, he offered us a broad smile and lots of apologies, informing us that sadly, the restaurant was closed on Sundays. He invited us however, to drive into the compound so that we could comfortably turn our cars around. No sooner had we driven onto the premises than Andrew the member of staff on duty, approached us. Andrew gave us a red carpet welcome in spite of the fact that the establishment was actually closed. He asked if it was our first visit and when we responded affirmatively, he apologized because they would not be able to serve us, handed us brochures and offered us a tour of the premises, which we accepted. This unexpected and warm treatment not only eliminated our disappointment, but also made us all the more eager to return to the casino's restaurant at our earliest opportunity. Warm welcomes make a lasting positive impression. Do your employees make customers feel so welcome that they are eager to return?

## Display enthusiasm

One morning as I approached my neighbourhood petrol station expecting the same undifferentiated, routine service that most petrol pump attendants seem to have mastered, I noticed the two female pump attendants jumping up and down enthusiastically. I pulled up in front of the more energetic of the two and asked her if there was a jumping competition going on. Gladys burst out laughing and responded "No, it's just our customer service!"

I watched Gladys very closely as she filled up the petrol tank, wrote a receipt for the transaction and cleaned my car's windshield. As she performed each task, she actually appeared to be enjoying herself. Her behaviour prompted me to ask her if she was a full time pump attendant

MAKE POSITIVE FIRST IMPRESSIONS

*Welcome warmly*

or if she was a desk officer, in the field for a day, just for the experience. Gladys assured me that she was indeed a pump attendant and proceeded to pitch the company's newest product - another type of unleaded petrol to be launched the following day.

Gladys' visible enthusiasm for her job made me a captive audience to her sales pitch. Furthermore, I ended up switching to the more expensive product she was promoting purely in response to her effervescence. What an asset Gladys is to her employer! Happy customers are more receptive to new product suggestions and much easier to sell more to. Your mood will affect the mood of customers doing business with you. An upbeat and positive staff will earn you more sales than employees who make it apparent that being at work feels like torture and having to deal with customers only makes matters worse. Make a positive and engaging attitude one of your hiring criteria for front line staff.

## Smile and work wonders

Eunice used to be a check-out clerk but now works in her supermarket's bakery. She is always in high spirits and seems to have a smile glued permanently to her face. Her smile is so infectious that everyone she interacts with walks away with a smile too. While Eunice was a check-out clerk, no matter how long the line at her register was, I happily joined the queue. Eunice's smile and warm reception always made me feel like I was the supermarket's only customer.

If only every business had a Eunice - someone whose cheery smile melts a customer's fatigue away while making each customer feel like they are the only customer who counts.

## Impress with a positive attitude

My organization is developing a project concept with the Faculty of Development Studies at one of our universities. As part of our preliminary discussions, Wendo a lecturer, travelled from Western Uganda to Eastern Uganda to visit our projects in that area. Wendo's trip began with a long bus ride from Western Uganda the day before our appointment.

The following day when we picked her up in a Kampala suburb, Wendo was in very high spirits, a mood that rubbed off on the rest of us, lasting all the way to our projects 80 kilometres away, throughout our visits to hot and dusty project sites and all the way back to Kampala.

Even when Wendo missed both the 5:00pm and 6:00pm buses back to her home town, her positive attitude did not falter. Once on the 7:00pm bus, she sent me a text message letting me know she would be home by midnight. Early the next morning I called her to see if she had arrived safely. Wendo was already at her desk, at work.

Wendo's sunny disposition and positive attitude make her an excellent ambassador for her faculty. Even personal inconvenience did not alter her mood. I wish there was a way to package and sell her positive, upbeat attitude to all our service providers. More common than employees with a positive attitude are the sulking employees who penalize customers for their unhappy circumstances. Have you spent any time at all, checking in to see what kind of attitude your employees portray to customers? Positive attitudes impress and draw customers back.

## Put customers at ease

How far do you go to put your customers at ease? For most people, visits to the doctor are anxiety-laden. My friend Maggie is no different, so she asked me to accompany her to see a specialist for a digital mammogram and ultrasound. Maggie's gynaecologist needed a specialist's opinion on the lump she had found while examining her. Expecting the worst, Maggie was a teary, nervous wreck by the time we arrived at the Imaging Centre.

A smiling uniformed guard welcomed us and showed us to the check-in counter where another smiling, gentle-mannered attendant signed Maggie in. A technician (our third smiling face that morning) walked us to an attractive waiting area with dim lighting, scented candles burning on a coffee table, and soft background music playing. "I love this place," a now tearless Maggie remarked, as she snuggled into the fluffy spa robe provided to keep her warm. "I feel completely at home!" To further lessen Maggie's diminishing anxiety, the medical personnel conducting the tests explained everything they were doing as they did it. The test results were available immediately and thankfully, Maggie had nothing to worry about.

That imaging centre created a soothing environment in which anxious patients are effectively calmed with kindness and compassion. Creating an ambience that puts your customers in the best frame of mind will encourage more customers to do business with you. Creating a suitable ambience for whatever business you are in does not have to be an expensive exercise. Just making sure your premises are clean, comfortable, uncluttered and orderly is a strong start.

## Treat all customers equally

Most of the times I have used our airport's frequent flyer lounge, I have noticed that beyond the initial warm greeting everyone receives from the gentleman at the door, there emerge two distinct categories of service: service reserved for people who are either known to be or look like VIPs and service (or lack of it) for the rest.

From my observations, as soon as a celebrity, highly visible public figure or distinguished looking foreigner sits down, a smiling waiter or waitress bearing a heated, damp washcloth for the VIP materializes, takes the VIP's order and delivers refreshments to the seated VIP. The other level of service reserved for non-VIPs like me, includes the individual sitting down for several minutes and finally realizing that if they are to have refreshments, they will need to walk to the counter, place their order, wait while it is assembled and then walk back to their seat with the ordered items.

I find it odd that there are clearly two levels of distinctly different service in a lounge that should treat all guests equally. The attentive service enjoyed by one group of customers should be available to every customer eligible to use that lounge. Unfortunately for travellers, there is only one frequent flyer lounge at this particular East African airport so a frequent flyer can either choose to do without lounge services or settle for the discriminatory services offered.

*Make customers feel comfortable*

Does your business offer two levels of service - one for those who appear not to have much money and another for those who appear to be financially endowed? Potential customers who receive cold treatment have absolutely no incentive to spend their money with you. If they have a choice, they will simply go elsewhere in search of a place where they feel welcome and appreciated.

## Treat customers with dignity

Stella is a loyal member of a Southern African airline's frequent flyer programme. When this airline joined the Star Alliance Global Airline Network, it assured its customers that they would continue receiving the same courtesy and respect they had grown accustomed to. It appears however, that some airlines that participate in that alliance are an exception.

While flying on another Star Alliance airline's flight from Johannesburg to Ndola, Stella was upgraded from economy to business class at check-in. As usual, before take-off the flight attendant served drinks to the business class passengers but when she got to Stella, she asked her for her boarding pass saying she needed to make sure Stella was a business class passenger. The flight attendant inspected Stella's boarding pass then instead of taking her drink order, walked away. At lunch time, the same flight attendant served business class lunches to everyone but Stella, who was handed an economy lunch box.

As a frequent flyer accustomed to preferential treatment, Stella was nothing less than dishonoured and completely humiliated. Why had that "sister" airline even bothered "upgrading" her? Upgrades are typically offered to demonstrate customer appreciation and include all the accompanying frills. By disregarding that, a flight attendant singlehandedly embarrassed a frequent flyer and made her feel like an unappreciated pariah. Customers and more especially loyal customers should be treated with dignity and made to feel so welcome that they want to voluntarily return. Stella vows never to use that particular Southern African airline ever again and tells every traveller she knows about her unpleasant experience at that airline's hands. Are customers who felt poorly treated telling anyone who will listen, negative stories about your business?

## Value your appearance

Victoria and I had dinner at a local Indian restaurant and we could not find fault with anything but the shoddy appearance of the waiters' uniforms, a slightly distracted waiter and a US$0.25 charge for takeaway boxes, all of which detracted from an otherwise pleasant experience.

Several months later my friends and I were back at the same restaurant, primarily because we knew the food there is consistently delicious. That evening, the atmosphere in the restaurant seemed very well-blended and relaxing. Wearing new and much better fitting uniforms, instead of standing out as an eyesore like they did before, the waiters in their brown uniforms actually looked like they belonged in that setting. Everything and everyone at the restaurant was aligned to create a pleasant dining experience in a relaxing environment. We ended up feeling so relaxed we actually worked our way through all the food we ordered and had no need to find out whether the $0.25 charge for each takeaway box had been dropped along with the old uniforms.

What image do your employees' appearances portray? Does your company appreciate the visual impact of employees' appearances on customers? Unkempt employee uniforms are unappealing, make a poor impression and do not attract new customers or keep old ones. As you pay attention to your business premises for that positive first impression, ensure that all your employees present a professional image. This restaurant aligned the appearance of employee uniforms with the image it seeks to portray.

When everything about your business reinforces your desired image, customers will respond positively, without even knowing why.


## Portray a professional image

Nicole was helping with her cousin's bridal party. The day before the wedding, eight bridesmaids' dresses still needed to be altered one last time. So Nicole escorted the nervous bridal party to the bridal boutique where the dresses were originally tailored.

Upon entering the premises, Nicole felt an immediate sense of calm, like the place had been deliberately decorated to soothe the jumpy nerves of flustered bridal parties. The gentle manner in which the staff approached, greeted and invited the bridal party to relax on the comfortable chairs provided for just that purpose, helped calm everyone down.

A few minutes later, the proprietor emerged, to gently advise the bridal party on their options at that late juncture. Although it was Friday night, there were no rude comments from the staff, no sour looks and no raised voices from anyone. Everyone including the proprietor worked efficiently, diligently and politely until 10:00pm when all the dresses were finally ready and a happy bridal party departed.

Think about your business. Is your staff calm (especially when dealing with anxious customers)? Do they handle customers in a professional manner? Do your business premises provide a complementary environment? These attributes will collaborate to successfully help customers through what can be a very stressful time. Consequently, not only will you stay in business; but your business will grow.

## Points to Ponder

1. What first impression does your business make on prospective customers? What thoughts go through the mind of a customer who enters your premises or visits your website for the first time?

2. How do you receive customers? Are they met by the smiling faces of employees happy to be at work or, are customers made to feel like nuisances and irritations?

3. Do your employees present a positive and professional first impression? If employees wear uniforms, are they in good condition?

4. Are your customers attended to promptly or do they end up leaving because nobody bothers to find out why they are there, or what they would like?

5. Have you ever thought about the sales revenue you lose when a customer walks out of your premises in protest, because service is non-existent, too slow or even rude?

6. Have you considered the cost of negative word-of-mouth to your business?

## To Do List

It will cost you nothing to consistently offer a smiling welcome, say hello and goodbye to every customer and next to nothing to keep the premises you occupy clean. The returns in terms of repeat customers and positive word of mouth however, are high.

- List three things your company will begin doing this week, to improve the first impression it makes. Now, implement them.

- Create and distribute a welcome and goodbye script to your team members. What would you like them to say to each and every customer who walks in? Ask your team members to suggest their own ideas. Once your company starts following the scripts, let your team members hold each other accountable for actually following the script.

## How Are You Doing?

If a principle is one that you currently practice, put a tick (√) in the Yes column. If a principle is one you need to work on, put a tick in the No column.

| **Make Positive First Impressions** | Yes | No |
|---|---|---|
| Exude a warm welcome | | |
| Display enthusiasm | | |
| Smile and work wonders | | |
| Impress with a positive attitude | | |
| Put customers at ease | | |
| Treat all customers equally | | |
| Treat customers with dignity | | |
| Value your appearance | | |
| Portray a professional image | | |

# CHAPTER 3
# BE COURTEOUS

Common courtesy is not that common after all, or so the saying goes. This is quite surprising since courtesy and decorum are traditional values across Africa. For some reason however, the values our parents took great pains to impart to us disappeared somewhere along the way. It is common for service providers to treat paying customers as though they are being given a free and undeserved service, at the service provider's expense. Grumpy faces, rude retorts, corner cutting and incredibly slow service are commonplace and well accepted. Beyond a smiling welcome, discerning customers expect to be treated with courtesy. Why then do customers who have options choose to continue supporting businesses that treat them as though they are doing them a favour? Thankfully, regionalization, globalization and increasing competition will eventually put a stop to this. Is your business ready for the shift of power from service providers to customers?

What gives any of your employees the right to treat any customer poorly? Day after day customer after customer either walks out of a business feeling non-consequential or hangs up a telephone in frustration over the unhelpful stance adopted by the customer service representative on the other side. Instead of being made to feel like the valuable individuals they are, the vast majority of customers in this part of the world are constantly made to feel like they do not count at all. It is possible that customers who have never had the pleasure of enjoying customer service in another part of the world have been numbed into accepting this type of almost abusive treatment at the hands of their service providers. Those days however, are fast coming to an end. The combination of the influx of competitors who know how to demonstrate that they value customers, the return to their home countries of nationals who have lived overseas and an increasingly more demanding younger generation entering the work force ensures that more pressure is gradually being brought to bear on service providers.

You will do well to make courtesy an attribute that your business or company is known for. Drum this into your employees at all levels. Reward employees for demonstrating courtesy at all times and even more, for maintaining a courteous stance when under pressure. Make an example of your more negative employees. Recognize that by keeping them on board in that negative state, you are lowering the morale of your entire staff and losing valuable sales from the potential or actual customers who simply choose to walk away. In their book *The Power of Nice, Linda Kaplan Thaler and Robin Koval*[v] say that rude gestures and remarks are like germs, they silently have an effect on you and everyone around you. As you might imagine, positive impressions have the opposite impact, giving off positive energy with a multiplier effect. Employees who are unable to respond to requests to change their negative attitudes should be invited to look for employment elsewhere before they cause irreparable damage to your business.

To help your employees deliver at the level you expect them to, you will need to create systems to help guide employee behaviour. The world famous Disney, has created service standards that support the delivery of their service theme. The four elements are Safety, Courtesy, Show and Efficiency[vi]. When faced with making multiple decisions that affect different areas of service at the same time, employees simply refer to their service standards and make decisions in the order prescribed. So for example, if a customer is behaving in a manner that puts other customers' safety at risk, the employee does what they need to in order to ensure everyone's safety first. In that scenario, courtesy to the customer who is out of line takes second place. Do your employees have a decision-making hierarchy to follow? If yes, is it well publicized? If no, there is no time like the present to start working on one.

Interestingly enough, although we are raised to treat other people the way we would like to be treated, given what I have seen about the way some people treat themselves, I sometimes feel the saying should be changed to say "Treat others the way they would like to be treated." Do you treat your customers the way they would like to be treated? Nobody likes it when they experience rude and disrespectful treatment, more so if it is at the hands of someone they are paying to provide them with goods or a service.

How does your business or company measure up on the courtesy-meter? If you are a front line employee, how do you treat customers? Are you an example that your fellow employees can and should follow, or do you need to make some changes to ensure that you keep your job and that your company remains in business? Beyond a smiling welcome, be attentive to all customers throughout their visit - not just the ones who look like they have plenty of money to spend. Politely listen and attend to their requests. Look customers in the eye when you speak to them. When they leave, thank them for stopping by and wish them a good morning, afternoon or evening, whatever the case may be.

## Make courtesy your hallmark

When vandals siphoned transformer oil from at least two of the electricity transformers in my home town, the surrounding areas (including my parents' home) experienced a black-out that lasted several days. Now, my father is one of those individuals who hardly ever complain about anything. On Day Four of the blackout however, even he could not take it any longer, so he visited the electricity company's local office for an update. Everyone in the first office my father entered was so busy that most of them ignored his greeting. Surprised at this rude display, my father raised his voice, informing everyone within earshot that they were culturally bound to respond to him, no matter how busy they were. A more enthusiastic response from the employees ensued. When my father asked for an update, one of the employees retorted that the community should be more vigilant in protecting the transformers. Realizing that he would not find any answers there, my father asked to see the manager.

In sharp contrast to the previous employee, the manager was polite and respectful, informing my father that it would be another two days before the black-out ended. Fortunately it was over the next day.

Every employee must be trained on how to handle customers courteously. Rude employees will ruin your company's reputation, costing you both customers and the revenue they bring. Beyond training, employees must subsequently be monitored, rewarded for meeting the required standards and pointed in the right direction when they fall short.

## Handle customers with care

Consider Jackie's interactions with our electricity provider for example. 08:45 - Jackie receives a distress call from home. A disconnection team unmoved by pleas of "You have not invoiced us for over three months!" is busy at work. Jackie immediately calls the provider to file a complaint about the unissued invoices and the disconnection. She then rushes to her bank and deposits US$100 on the provider's bank account and dispatches payment proof to the provider's local office.

13:00 - Jackie calls customer service again, only to be castigated by Baker for not following up on a warning text message that the provider sent to her landline! Text messages to landlines since when was this possible? Taken aback, Jackie asks Baker to update his records with her mobile phone number. 18:00 - With no feedback from the provider, Jackie makes call three. Jane issues Jackie a new reference number, after scolding her for filing her first complaint incorrectly. Irritated and dreading the dark night ahead, Jackie asks to speak to Jane's supervisor. Jane reports that Supervisor Eva is busy but will return Jackie's call shortly. As expected, the call never came!

Do your services leave customers desperately wishing for an alternative? Not delivering invoices yet disconnecting service, sending text messages to a landline, being rude to an already unhappy customer and not returning calls only result in growing numbers of incredibly unhappy customers. Instead, invoice on time and make sure invoices are actually delivered, send text messages if you must, to mobile telephones, not to landlines this is easy to tell simply from looking at the number itself.

# KEEPING CUSTOMERS

*Extend courtesy*

Offer polite, courteous service to querying customers and return calls if you promise to. Sound simple? These simple and affordable actions yield disproportionately high returns. Why do we find them so difficult to carry out?

## Serve with pleasure

We have all shopped there - the supermarket where the shop attendants seem to be paid to sit around chatting in groups, with their backs to shopping customers. Juliet found herself in just that kind of supermarket. She was looking for golden syrup and try as she might, she could not get an attendant's attention. Finally, she walked over to where an attendant was sitting, just to get her attention.

"Do you have golden syrup?" Juliet asked. Without even bothering to look at her, let alone get off her seat, the attendant responded "No." The manner in which she responded was so unconvincing, that Juliet opted to walk up and down each aisle on her own, to confirm that there was indeed no golden syrup. Several aisles later, she stumbled upon the syrup section, so she walked back to the attendant and asked her to come and see where the syrup was shelved. When Juliet pointed to the syrup on the shelf, instead of apologizing, the attendant insisted, in a raised voice, that Juliet had asked her for something different.

Eagerness to serve, an apology and a smile were all it would have taken to turn that negative experience into a positive one for Juliet. Instead, Juliet vowed never to return. A lost customer over something so simple!

## Listen respectfully

One morning, before heading to a Christian bookshop to compare prices, Sally had started out at one of Kampala's largest bookshops. Upon entering the large bookshop, Sally had informed an attentive shop attendant that she was looking for a King James Version (KJV) of the Bible. The pleasant attendant had then personally escorted Sally to the Christian Religious Education section and made sure Sally was comfortable before returning to her work station.

# KEEPING CUSTOMERS

*Listen respectfully*

Two particular Bibles caught Sally's attention that morning: a large black, leather bound KJV at US$25 and a medium size imitation leather KJV that included a dictionary and study help at US$9. In a bid to find better prices and possibly more variety of choice, Sally headed downstairs to a Christian bookstore. Upon perusing the Bible section, Sally was surprised to find that many of the Bibles on display cost over US$50. Not one to give up however, Sally looked to see if she could find the two Bibles that had caught her eye earlier in the first bookshop. Sure enough, the Christian bookshop had an exact copy of one of the leather bound Bibles. The only difference was the price tag, it cost $8 more in the Christian bookshop. The shop attendant responded to Sally's inquiry about the price difference with a blank stare.

Not one to hold back customer feedback, Sally proceeded to ask the attendant to let her manager know that just a flight of stairs away, another bookshop carried the same Bible for $8 less. How did the attendant respond to this useful information? She turned her back on Sally and walked away leaving Sally giving the rest of her feedback to the books on the shelves. Sally quickly retraced her steps and ended up back at the first bookshop where she was happy to purchase a reasonably priced KJV in a more welcoming environment. Courteous, polite service will always bring customers back to you.

How many establishments lose out on valuable information and potential sales simply because they choose to treat customers with disdain? Attendants must be courteous and attentive and should be trained to view customer remarks as a goldmine of valuable information for the business. Encourage your team members to report all customer remarks to a central point. This could be a supervisor, responsible for recording all remarks and recommending ways in which your company might use those remarks to the company's advantage.

## Show customers you value them

One of my American volunteers fell sick and had to be admitted to a Kampala hospital. The nurses promised that a private room would be available the following day so Megan spent her first night in a ward. The next morning, I asked two junior nurses at the outpatient desk who I

# KEEPING CUSTOMERS

*Manage unruly customers*

should consult about Megan's move. They pointed to an older sister. Before I could even utter a word, the sister snapped at me, referring me to the junior nurses. "They sent me to you," I replied. "What is it?" was the brusque rejoinder, as she continued reading. "How do I get my patient moved?" The irritated reply: "I don't know. Ask in the ward."

That afternoon, the sister who had earlier acted too busy to help me, wanted to know who would pay Megan's bill. When she learned I was responsible, she immediately demanded a deposit. To my assurances that I would not whisk Megan away before paying, the sister retorted "It is hospital policy," triggering an uncharitable response from me as I walked away.

That nurse should never have made a contributor to her salary feel like an unappreciated, irritating nuisance. Instead, she ought to have dropped whatever she was doing to find out what I needed from her that morning and found me the information I was looking for.

Had she treated me courteously, I would have been happy to hand over a deposit later that afternoon in compliance with "Hospital Policy." In order to enjoy a minor victory of my own however, I avoided that nurse for the duration of Megan's hospital stay and did not make any payments towards the bill until Megan was finally discharged. What kind of rebellious behaviour do your employees cause customers to adopt? Customers who are treated courteously will respond in a similar fashion and the reverse.

## Handle unruly customers firmly

Brenda was in the fast lane at her supermarket, hoping to quickly pay for the air freshener she needed and continue with her errands. As the cashier was ringing up the items purchased by the couple just ahead of her, the cashier found that some of the items required barcode verification. This exercise took the cashier several minutes, causing an irate man at the very back of the queue to stomp his way to the front and attempt to bully the cashier into scanning his packet of shaving razors, ahead of the couple being served at the time.

To her credit, and to the immense relief of the other waiting customers, the cashier calmly invited the irate customer to return to his position at the back of the queue. Even the string of obscenities that the customer then spewed at the cashier had no effect on her demeanor. The customer stormed away angrily, leaving his packet of shaving razors on the counter.

Bravo to the cashier for standing her ground and for not accommodating one loud, obnoxious and demanding individual at the expense of several other customers patiently waiting to be served. Although the irate bully walked away unhappy, the rest of the customers were quite pleased that the cashier had put the bully in his place. Employees should ensure that no one, not even a customer, disrupts the flow of service for their customers unnecessarily. Have you provided your employees with a decision-making hierarchy that guides them in deciding how to behave in different situations? What could possibly take priority over an irritated, loud and obnoxious customer demanding to be served ahead of everyone else in line?

## Exercise courtesy and efficiency

Following a disappointing stop in an international airline's licensed agent office, I had to rush to a meeting with my travel plans still incomplete. When my meeting ended, instead of following the less than polite licensed agent's advice that I drive back into the city centre in order to consult the airline office, I simply called the airline. I needed to find out if my inquiry could be handled over the phone.

In sharp contrast to my earlier experience with the airline's licensed agent, the airline's customer service representative sounded happy to talk to me. I could almost hear the smile in her voice. She listened to my inquiry, carefully explained why some changes had been made to my air ticket and even gave me some tips on how I could obtain the additional changes I was looking for after I commenced my journey - definitely a solution provider.

Every time I have interacted with that airline's customer service representatives, in person or on the phone, I have found them to be courteous, efficient, solution-oriented individuals who leave me smiling. I look forward to all my interactions with them. Do your customers say the same thing about you?

## Display professionalism even under pressure
I received a desperate phone call on a Friday at 9.30am from two colleagues in India who were at the Uganda High Commission in New Delhi, applying for visas. They needed confirmed hotel reservations to be faxed to the High Commission by 10:30am Uganda time, when the High Commission would be closing. They planned to fly out of Delhi the following Tuesday. After the call, it took me 30 minutes to get to town. With only 30 minutes left and a constant barrage of frantic text messages from my colleagues in New Delhi, I got to their chosen hotel.

Feeling the full weight of the pressure from my colleagues, I did my best to be pleasant to the Reservations Agent, explaining the urgency of the situation.

At one time or another, we have all been the recipients of deliberately slow service from a person who simply wants to demonstrate that they, not you, hold "the power." My situation was perfect for this. I desperately needed something in a hurry and was exerting undue pressure on the service provider. She however was clearly not flustered. She handled my request professionally and efficiently in spite of my unhelpful and frequent interferences and succeeded in faxing the hotel confirmations to my friends in New Delhi before their 10:30am deadline. Both my friends and I obtained what we were looking for and will definitely keep that hotel on our list of preferred places to stay.

## Exude a pleasant attitude
My laptop's motherboard was damaged after a fall. Unfortunately, I was not even able to retrieve my data from my backup files because the portable hard drive I had saved them to, converted them into a file format I did not have the software to read. Someone recommended a technician called Hashim to fix the laptop. Hashim ran several tests and noted that the motherboard had to be written off. On the bright side however, the hard drive seemed intact and all he had to do was find a way to retrieve and transfer the data to another device.

For three days Hashim was in our office for several hours, trying different data retrieval methods. Each day, 9:30pm was the earliest he left the premises and always with a smile. Finally, on Saturday (day four) Hashim found a data retrieval method that worked.

Granted, four days felt like an incredibly long time to have to wait for vital data. On the plus side however, Hashim's consistently positive attitude, pleasant manner, perseverance and total dedication to the task throughout its duration are highly commendable. For his attitude, not his speed, he will be the person we will call the next time we need help with one of our electronic devices. Do your employees cause similar feelings of loyalty within your customer base?

## Points to Ponder

1. Do you treat every one of your customers courteously?

2. How do you ensure that all your employees treat all your customers courteously?

3. Do you reward employees for consistently courteous behaviour?

4. What consequences, if any, does an employee who is rude to customers face?

5. What measures do you take to help correct that employee's behaviour?

6. How do you compensate customers who let you know they felt slighted by the manner in which they were treated?

## To Do List

- At your next staff meeting, invite your employees to share personal experiences, highlighting how they felt when someone they were buying something from was rude to them. How did they feel? What do they wish the rude person had done instead? How will they avoid duplicating that behaviour at your place of business?

- Invite your employees to create a contest in which they watch each other's performance with customers. What behaviour will win a prize and how often? Name the prize and determine how behaviour that does not meet the standard will be handled.

## How Are You Doing?

If a principle is one that you currently practice, put a tick (√) in the Yes column. If a principle is one you need to work on, put a tick in the No column.

| Be Courteous | Yes | No |
|---|---|---|
| Make courtesy your hallmark | | |
| Handle customers with care | | |
| Serve with pleasure | | |
| Listen respectfully | | |
| Show customers you value them | | |
| Handle unruly customers firmly | | |
| Exercise courtesy and efficiency | | |
| Display professionalism under pressure | | |
| Exude a pleasant attitude | | |

# CHAPTER 4
# PRACTICE HONESTY

Honesty was once a valued and admirable quality. Parents used to hammer it into their children and business owners did everything they could to ensure that their businesses were known for honest practices. Today however, it would seem that honesty is no longer viewed as being valuable. The media is replete with stories of unscrupulous leaders setting a bad example by misappropriating tremendously large sums of "free money," with impunity. One constantly encounters individuals trying to get their hands on money they have done nothing to earn. As many as can get away with it find a way of including an undeserved personal surcharge for services rendered. Why is it so difficult for all employees to remain honest in all dealings and for enterprises to monitor the integrity with which their services are provided?

Whenever possible, attach a price tag to items, visibly display a price list or have a printed price list readily available (e.g. a restaurant menu) so customers will know exactly how much they are supposed to pay for your product or service. Your price list should also include a request that customers insist on official receipts. By official receipts, I am not referring to the generic carbon copy-less receipt books that can be bought from any stationery shop. Rather, official receipts are generated by a register. If handwritten, they should include the company's official name and in some countries, the company Tax Identification Number as well as a carbon copy. These measures will lower the incidence of employees cheating in your business. They will also assure your customers that they are paying the correct amount for products and that the money they pay is going to the right place. To further ensure that all funds collected actually get deposited in the company coffers and not in the pockets of unscrupulous employees, although a slow way to conduct business, in the absence of an electronic register some establishments resort to having one person collect cash payments and hand all cash received to a different person who then prepares the receipt that is handed to the customer.

A truly loyal customer will not stoop so low as to accept the offer that your employee whispers into their ear, offering the same service the business offers, but at a lower price. Nor will a truly loyal customer ask your employee to do something for them off the books, for example, asking your employee to come after hours to repair the photocopier whose guarantee expired six months ago. So cultivate customer loyalty through the manner that you treat your customers.

If a customer asks you to do something that you know is well beyond what your company can deliver, rather than deceiving your customer by agreeing to undertake a task you know you cannot complete, let the customer know you will not be able to help. Do not however, stop there. In the interests of building your company's reputation as a solution provider, go the next step and give the customer some options to choose from. For instance, do you know another provider who can provide the service the customer is looking for? If yes, offer to make a call to the provider, inquiring as to whether they can accommodate your customer's request. Your customer will thank you for it and so will the provider who receives your call. Referring the business you cannot handle to someone else is an excellent way of building synergistic relationships within the business community, while helping your customer meet their objectives.

Set yourself apart by ensuring that your customers do not get cheated. If you successfully cheat a customer, that is nothing to celebrate. It is not your lucky day and in any event, it will soon catch up with you and you will be found out. Decline customer bribes, which will only compromise what you offer. Commit yourself to honesty. Always charge the right price and not a price that allows you to skim off "the difference." Strive to be reliable and dependable, always doing what you say you will. This could well be the difference that sets you apart from the competition.

## Delight with honesty

Unexpected honesty, how refreshing! Aware that I always hire the same driver for my frequent upcountry trips, my friend Stella suggested I "broaden my scope." Stella gave me Patrick's phone number, assured me that he was a conscientious driver and insisted that I would get amazing rates. Sure enough, Patrick's quote came in US$20 lower than my regular driver's.

Excited about the savings that switching to Patrick would entail, I eagerly awaited our first trip. On the appointed day, Patrick had a family emergency so he sent a replacement driver. The replacement driver turned out to have a road sign reading weakness, resulting in a speeding ticket which consumed the bulk of the fees he had expected to earn from the trip. Aware that our vehicle was running low on fuel and that the driver had next to no money left, and afraid of getting stranded en-route, I offered to purchase some fuel. After learning of our predicament, an apologetic Patrick monitored the rest of the trip by phone.

Two weeks later, Patrick delivered my fuel reimbursement and an additional US$10 which he said he owed me because I had travelled in a smaller car than his quote had referenced. Patrick's honesty, especially concerning something I was unaware of deeply impressed me. With non-speeding drivers, he will enjoy my business for many years to come. Do you come forward and let customers know when you have inadvertently charged them more than they were supposed to pay? Your honesty will only bind your customers even closer to you.

## Be consistently honest

Do the charlatans among us escalate their game for the festive season? On my way upcountry one holiday, I stopped on Main Street in a small town and walked into a shop where I spent no more than ten minutes. Upon returning to my vehicle, I asked Dennis the street parking attendant how much I owed for parking. US$0.25 was his enthusiastic response. Apparently, over Christmas, street parking in that town is more expensive than parking in the City of Kampala and cash (instead of the standard parking tickets) is an acceptable form of settlement. Knowing exactly what Dennis was up to, I asked him to sell me a strip of five parking tickets instead. The small town I was in is a frequent stop for me so, that US$0.50 would certainly be a good investment. Dennis' Christmas price however, was US$0.75. To sweeten the deal, he offered to let me off without giving him any parking tickets for parking on the street that morning. Laughing hard and wondering how many travellers had fallen victim to him, I let Dennis know that I would pay just US$0.50 for the tickets and use one for my parking fee. He offered no argument and did not even flinch when I asked him why he was acting dishonestly.

Why is it that some service-providers seek to take advantage of those they assume do not know any better? Dennis was trying to steal from both his employer and me. Have you found a way to accurately monitor the amounts of money your employees ask customers for?

## Demonstrate professional conduct

Upon the recommendation of one of the tenants in our office building, I contacted a freelance sign maker called Andrew. In each of our pre-contract meetings he demonstrated lots of energy and enthusiasm. I briefed Andrew on the job at hand and asked him several questions which he answered knowledgeably. Andrew clinched the deal when he mentioned that he had just become a partner in a firm that belongs to a friend of mine. Andrew even went as far as later providing a job estimate on my friend's company letterhead as proof of association.

Believing Andrew had understood exactly what I wanted (in terms of aesthetics and quality) and that he would indeed deliver the signs we had reviewed on his laptop several times, I confidently made a 50 per cent down payment. From that point on, Andrew's initial energy and enthusiasm were transformed into over three months of unreturned phone calls, missed appointments and unfulfilled promises to invite me to a press check. The garish excuses for signs that he finally abandoned at our doorstep (we refused to accept them) were printed in fading ink, included typos, and were clumsily adhered to poorly welded and rusty metal frames. Worse still, Andrew had the audacity to inform one of my colleagues that a larger company in town was the only firm capable of doing what we wanted. Why had this not come up earlier? He promised to refund our 50 per cent deposit and then simply disappeared.

KEEPING CUSTOMERS

Andrew completely misrepresented his capabilities, created imaginary links to my friend's firm, became unreachable and finally, abandoned his property - the garish signs we had rejected - at my office. Be professional in your conduct and demonstrate integrity. If you are unable to provide a customer with exactly what they are asking you for, tell them as much and let them make the decision to stay or go. Your honesty will draw them back even though they may have to look elsewhere for that particular project.

## Play above board

One of the Community Based Organizations (CBOs) I volunteer with in upcountry Jinja ordered seven exotic goats (to begin a breeding programme) from a farmers' association in another up country town, Mbale. Between order placement and collection, Robert, the association's chairman repeatedly assured the CBO that the animals were available and in good health. Representatives from the CBO therefore hired a vehicle and travelled 220 kilometres from Jinja to Mbale to purchase and collect the seven goats. Robert took the CBO team all over Mbale District (over eight hours of travel) in a seemingly random search in the hills for the goats he had claimed were available. By 8:00pm, only six of the seven ordered animals had been obtained and the CBO team had to return to Jinja, one animal short.

Contrary to standard breeding practices, four of the six goats were not tagged (casting doubt on their origin) and one of them looked quite emaciated. Additionally, Robert did not provide the team with any animal records (critical for breeding programmes) or a receipt for funds received. Instead, he wrote a note acknowledging receipt of funds and promised to post both the animal records and an official receipt later. As if that was not enough, Robert convinced the CBO team to pay for his Mbale room and board that night.

The entire purchase was fraught with irregularities. In my opinion, Robert clearly took advantage of a naive CBO team and fulfilled their longstanding order unsatisfactorily. Instead, Robert should have done everything in his power to deliver exactly what he had promised in exactly the way he had promised. Do you and your employees keep your word? Do your customers believe you will deliver what you promise to, in the promised fashion?

## Tell the truth about your products

Are your products what you claim they are? Leonard purchased what he was told was a brand new genuine leather laptop bag from a shop in one of Kampala's shopping malls. While in the shop, Leonard engaged the shop manager in a lively conversation which ended with her inviting Leonard to return in a few weeks when leather cleaning kits would be available. Because the laptop bag was in sealed packaging labelled "Pierre Cardin," Leonard opted to save the pleasure of viewing his purchase for the office. Once back at work, Leonard eagerly summoned some colleagues to witness the unveiling. Excited anticipation soon turned into shouts of dismay as Leonard's hand emerged from the packaging holding cracked straps attached to a bag with frayed edges. Clearly the bag was second-hand and certainly not made of leather. Disappointed, Leonard immediately returned the bag to the shop where he had purchased it. In spite of the shop manager agreeing that the bag had indeed been purchased there, she boldly denied Leonard a refund because he did not have a receipt. Surely, the lady could not have already forgotten the talkative customer she had served less than two hours earlier.

Pretending to sell genuine leather products and boldly denying Leonard, a cheated customer, his refund is behaviour to be frowned upon. Tell the truth about the products you are selling, so disappointed customers will not need to return items to you. Should the items be returned for not being what you claimed they were, do the honourable thing and either replace the product or give the customer a full refund. How do you respond when a customer reports that your product or your service did not meet expectations?

## Offer genuine service

I drive a 15 year old car, which renders my mechanic's number one of my most frequently dialled. Tired of this situation, I finally decided to take my car to the national dealership where the mechanics are supposed to

## KEEPING CUSTOMERS

*Be honest*

## PRACTICE HONESTY

be experts on that particular brand. After the smiling customer service representative took down the particulars of my vehicle and the problems I was having, she informed me in a conspiratorial whisper that my car was on the old side and the company preferred to service newer models. She advised me to try an "outside mechanic" and if I did not have one, she could recommend a garage run by one of the company's mechanics. I must have been walking in some kind of naïve reverie when I agreed to try the garage she recommended. Several hundred thousand shillings, missed appointments and lost tempers later, I finally got my car back. When I drove it home however, I noticed the car was making all kinds of new wheezing, creaking and whirring sounds. Upon getting a second opinion from a trusted vehicle expert who tested the parts that had been installed in my car, I learned that the recommended garage ran by so-called experts, had installed malfunctioning parts.

Clearly, I had been conned into participating in a scam that those employees run parallel to their jobs. Companies should have codes of conduct for their employees that eliminate this type of conflict of interest. Companies should further subject apprehended offenders to serious consequences, when in violation. In my case, when the company that employs the mechanic learned of my grievance, that was the end of the story. No apology, no compensation and no action taken against the mechanic. And to answer your question, I will never return to that dealership. Do you chase customers away by not addressing situations where you do not meet expectations?

## Make true claims

How many times has a shop attendant attempted to convince you that the prices offered in the shop where he/she works are the lowest available? And how many times after conducting a survey of your own, have you found their claims not to be true? When I had to purchase a large amount of hardware supplies for an upcountry construction project, I surveyed several local hardware shops. In one of the shops, the Marketing Manager Videsh challenged me to find a single reputable hardware supplier who could beat him on price. I was not able to. For each item I surveyed, this particular store's prices were anywhere up to

*Offer genuine service*

US$1.50 lower than the competition. This yields substantial "savings" when one is buying in bulk. When I had a construction emergency at the project site one weekend and could not get upcountry right away, Videsh allowed the builders to take the necessary materials from the shop on credit.

What lessons can we learn from this? First, unlike so many others, Videsh's price claims were actually true. Second, the credit facility he extended to this grateful customer absolutely guarantees that I will go to him for all my upcountry hardware needs. Are the price claims your business makes true?

## Display correct pricing

A friend of mine asked me to buy her a diaper bag. I had no trouble finding this particular supermarket's diaper bag section and no trouble reading all the shelf price tags, clearly displayed under each type of bag. The bags priced at US$9 looked good to me so I selected one and headed for the check-out lanes. When the glum-faced check-out clerk scanned the bag, its price came up as US$10.50. In response to my inquiry as to why the check-out price was different from the shelf price, the glum faced clerk turned to ask her sulking supervisor for an explanation. The sulking supervisor informed us both (with disdain, I might add), that the price of the bag had gone up but the shelf price tags had not yet been changed.

In Marketing we have a term for that -"bait and switch". Bait customers with a low advertised price and charge them a higher price at purchase. A "helpful" clerk on hearing the exchange ran back to the shelf to verify the price. According to her, the diaper bag I bought (of which there was an entire facing) did not actually have a shelf price tag. The only available price was the price in the system. Shoppers should never encounter differences between shelf and check-out prices. Retailers should be vigilant about making sure price tags on items and on shelves reflect the correct pricing. In cases where the shelf price is lower than the check-out price, the customer should not be forced to pay for the retailer's negligence. The displayed price ought to be honoured.

## Honour displayed prices

Belinda is a regular customer at her car washing bay in Kampala and even has a favourite "car-washer". At the washing bay, highly visible price charts clearly display the charges for various services e.g. small cars: US$2.50; big cars: US$3.00 etc. Belinda has a small car, so according to the price chart a car wash should cost her US$2.50.

This one time, however, Belinda drove to the washing bay and was disappointed to find that her favourite car-washer was not there. Her attempts to get someone else to wash her car initially proved futile because the available attendants were unwilling to work for just the clearly displayed $2.50. One of them even informed Belinda that for that amount, no one at the washing bay would even touch her car. How much more was she willing to offer? After plenty of begging and pleading, Belinda finally convinced one of the reluctant attendants to wash her car for the displayed price.

Do your employees reduce regular customers to beggars in a bid to secure clearly displayed pricing? You might need to have a price monitor in place, just to make sure your customers pay nothing more than the prices they are supposed to pay.

## Keep your word

A group of friends had missed a number of Uganda jazz musician Isaiah Katumwa's performances in Kampala. They were therefore particularly excited to find that they would all be in town on the night he was launching "Another Step". When purchasing the tickets, Raymond asked the young lady selling them whether she had a seating chart to enable guests choose their seats. She did not have one but assured him that all the seats were equally good. When he insisted on some kind of guarantee she promised to talk to her supervisor. The next day, Clare informed Raymond that her supervisor had agreed to hold three seats for his group and gave him a number to call upon arrival at the concert. Indeed when Raymond and his friends entered the concert hall, Clare was on hand to lead the group to the best seats in the house, where there was nothing to distract them as Isaiah Katumwa treated his audience to much more than their money's worth of his amazing talent.

Clare and her team placed such high value on customer satisfaction, that they kept their word and creatively and cheerfully accommodated a complete stranger's request for excellent seats. Raymond and his friends had nothing but rave reviews for both Isaiah's performance and the services rendered by his support staff. Do you endeavour to fulfil customer requests, even the unusual ones? And once you pledge to fulfil a request, do you follow through or does every pledge give you cause to keep your mobile phone off, rendering you unreachable?

## Deliver what you promise

How many of you will not believe what a service provider promises until you actually get it? Chances are that is because you have been disappointed so many times that you have become cynical. A few months ago, my satellite television provider agreed to put my account on hold for several weeks while I was away. Upon my return, I called the company expecting one of three responses - my request was never processed; my request was processed but the person on the phone either did not know how to; or was not authorized to reactivate my account. To my delighted surprise however, Mercy reinstated the service as we spoke and even told me my new subscription renewal date. A few days later however, the service was off. Believing that what I had thought to be excellent customer service was too good to be true after all, I called the company again. Mercy assured me it was a simple matter of her resetting my account, and indeed it was.

I was surprised to find a company that actually delivered exactly what it promised. And kudos to Mercy for her calm, customer-oriented phone manner. Why was I so surprised? Should delivery as promised not be the norm? How has your business contributed to causing customers to believe that companies and their employees hardly ever do what they say they will?

## Observe expiry dates

Shoppers generally expect that the stock in the shops they visit is responsibly rotated and that expired products are promptly removed from the shelves. I purchased several packets of henna powder in a shop in Minnesota, USA. After leaving the shop however, I found that every single packet had an expiry date that was over a year ago. So I returned the expired henna to the shop. To her credit, the shop attendant immediately gave me a full refund and told me the expired product would be destroyed and replaced.

A week later, I returned to the same shop, looking to buy some freshly stocked henna. I was astounded to find however, that not only was the expired henna prominently displayed, but worse still, the expiry dates had been blacked out with a marker.

Intentionally attempting to trick unsuspecting customers into purchasing expired products is simply dishonest. Instead, do all you can to move products off the shelf well before their expiry date. You might even consider holding a "buy one, get one free" promotion months before the products expire. This would provide a superior alternative to having to destroy everything after the expiry date, which is what responsible retailers do. How does your company handle expired stock?

PRACTICE HONESTY

*Run an honest business*

## Points to Ponder

1. Are honesty and integrity values that your business upholds?

2. How have you visibly demonstrated the importance you attach to honesty and integrity to your employees or team mates?

3. If you do value honesty and integrity, what are you doing to ensure that your employees also embrace those values in all their dealings?

4. How do you ensure that your customers are not paying more than they are supposed to?

5. What are you doing to discourage customers from paying underhanded employees instead of your company, a little less than your published prices for the very same product or service you offer?

6. If you cannot provide a product or service that a customer is looking for, how do you handle the customer's request?

## To Do List

- This week, find a way to conspicuously display your prices to customers.

- Post a sign that asks your customers to insist on receiving an official receipt.

- What other information do you need to display for your customers' attention?

## How Are You Doing?

If a principle is one that you currently practice, put a tick (√) in the Yes column. If a principle is one you need to work on, put a tick in the No column.

|  | Yes | No |
|---|---|---|
| **Practice Honesty** | | |
| Delight with honesty | ☐ | ☐ |
| Be consistently honest | ☐ | ☐ |
| Demonstrate professional conduct | ☐ | ☐ |
| Play above board | ☐ | ☐ |
| Tell the truth about your products | ☐ | ☐ |
| Offer genuine service | ☐ | ☐ |
| Make true claims | ☐ | ☐ |
| Display correct pricing | ☐ | ☐ |
| Honour displayed prices | ☐ | ☐ |
| Keep your word | ☐ | ☐ |
| Deliver what you promise | ☐ | ☐ |
| Observe expiry dates | ☐ | ☐ |

# CHAPTER 5
# JUST DO YOUR JOB

Whenever a customer walks in the door or visits your online retail website, they have a set of expectations. When a customer walks into a supermarket to purchase an item and cannot find it, they expect to find an attendant who will politely listen to their query and then either show them exactly where the item is located or let them know that your particular supermarket does not carry what they are looking for. When a customer asks for information on something, they expect the employee they are addressing to have an answer. If I come in for a meal, I expect to get a meal. The people who are paid to offer a service however, often act as if simple requests in line with what they do for a living are nothing short of punishments; and expecting those employees to do what they are paid to do is plainly put, a bridge too far. The businesses that will emerge winners in this increasingly competitive global marketplace are the businesses whose employees are not only passionate about doing their job, but are also solution- oriented and willing to go the extra mile too.

Who do you have working for you? Did your employees enter the company through a proper recruiting process or, are you saddled with family and friends who do not have the right credentials for the job and therefore do not deliver as expected, yet insist on acting as though they did you a favour by agreeing to come and work with you? If you fall in this category, you owe it to your company to train the employees who do not have the right qualifications and thus equip them to perform. Your other option is to ask anyone who is unable to meet the required performance standards to leave.

Anyone who deals with customers but finds it difficult to go the extra mile, should at a minimum, simply deliver what customers expect. In other words, at least meet customer expectations. If you are an employer who is happy to settle for employees who simply meet expectations however, I have news for you - you are about to go out of business! Employees that fall into that category will more often than not waste valuable energy and time thinking of creative ways to put in the minimum possible effort, for the minimum acceptable results. The word "excellence" is far from their vocabulary and it follows that it will be far from your company too.

Do your employees actually know what is expected of them? Have they gone through an orientation programme introducing them to the way things are expected to work in your company as well as clearly informing them of their specific roles? You would be surprised to learn of the number of employees who have to stumble their way through their job, with little to no guidance whatsoever. Once your employees know what is expected of them, they will inevitably have to undergo some kind of training.

Regardless of whether you run a large or small company, it is imperative that you invest in training employees to meet your desired and hopefully well communicated standards. If you are not able to sponsor employees to attend training programmes off site, design your own in-house training programmes with you or another senior employee conducting the training. Training may also be conducted on the job, in one-on-one sessions. Every once in a while, invite an anonymous mystery shopper to visit your business and document their entire interaction with your staff. This will help you assess whether or not the training you provide is actually changing employee behaviour. Remember that for adult learners, experiential training with plenty of class participation in the form of exercises, role plays and case studies will have a stronger, sustainable impact.

If you are a front line employee who interfaces with customers all day long, every day, and you cannot drum up enough passion to simply do your job with a smile, your supervisor may not have said this to you yet, but it is definitely time for you to think about finding something you

JUST DO YOUR JOB

*Do what you are paid for*

enjoy doing. Remove yourself from a service oriented environment if it is not the environment for you. Ask your supervisor to reassign you to a position that does not interact with customers, or leave. You are hurting more than helping your employer if you cannot muster the enthusiasm to simply do your job, with a smile.

## Display professional conduct

It was taking the airline agent checking in a client for a flight quite some time to complete the exercise. He kept on having to ask the agents on either side for help. Realizing that the young man was new on the job, Jessica was patient. After Jessica had been waiting for 15 minutes at the counter, a more seasoned agent came to the rescue. She quickly took care of everything, explaining each step to the struggling young man and printing Jessica's boarding passes and baggage tag. All the young man had to do was attach the baggage tag to the client's suitcase. This however was not to happen because the young man appeared to have developed a hearing defect. Twice, the rescuing agent asked him to attach the baggage tag. And twice, right there in full customer view, the young man sat perfectly still, looked straight ahead and pretended the rescuing agent was talking to herself. Fortunately, she quickly realized what she was dealing with, tagged the suitcase herself and apologized to the client for the young man's behaviour.

Obviously the new recruit squandered a learning opportunity; more importantly however, his rude response to someone who was helping him (an all too common practice), in full customer view, was simply unprofessional. Instead, the young man ought to have demonstrated a willingness to learn by paying attention and going on to thank his rescuer with a generous smile. Finally, he should have apologized to the client for the unnecessary delay. Do you encourage your employees to display professional conduct at all times?

## Follow through to the end

On one of my trips from Maputo to Entebbe via Johannesburg, I got home two whole days ahead of my suitcase. The Saturday night I landed, a very pleasant and polite airport handling services agent explained the baggage tracing process to me and confirmed that my suitcase would indeed be delivered to the delivery address I indicated. Though impressed by Ruth's customer service, I remained sceptical about the handling service promise to deliver my suitcase to an address 15 kilometres outside the city.

By midday that Monday, my suitcase had not been delivered so I called the handling service for an update, only to learn that my file had been closed because my suitcase had been dropped off. But no one had bothered to tell me. I politely asked for the phone number of the driver who "dropped off" my suitcase and upon reaching him, learned that he attempted to deliver my suitcase to the designated address earlier on, but was forced to leave the suitcase at the airline's city office. Why? When he got to the address and called my number, the man who answered the phone did not know me. The driver advised me to follow up with the airline and collect my suitcase from their city office.

Needless to say, I was not impressed by the driver's brand of customer service. If he had indeed driven all the way to the designated address - which I doubt - why was a phone call his only attempt to gain entry to the premises? Had he actually driven to my home, at a minimum, he should have at least hooted to draw our attention to the gate. The driver was happy to delegate his incomplete assignment to this customer, without even pro-actively informing me of the decision he had taken. How sure are you that your employees see assignments through to the end?

## Be diligent
Six weeks after asking his bank to reverse a double debit, Derrick still had not received any updates. Tired of waiting for the elusive call that was supposed to confirm that his account had been credited, Derrick finally made a trip to his local branch to follow-up. When the branch manager checked his account online, she confirmed that the credit had not yet been made. So she called the clerk responsible at another bank location. It turned out that the clerk had been transferred to a third branch and had left for her new appointment before adjusting the account. To the

branch manager's credit, she tracked down the errant clerk and asked how far she had gone with the adjustment.

Derrick listened to the ensuing conversation (albeit one-sided) in captive amazement. The person on the other side of the phone gave a litany of excuses for not having done her job - not knowing how to make reversals, not knowing where to get filed vouchers, being transferred and finally, not knowing the client's telephone number (which is listed in the bank's database). The manager addressed each excuse and proceeded to cajole the voice on the other side to do the right thing.

Are junior staffers so secure in their jobs these days that they can pick and choose which customer requests to fulfil, and even debate with their supervisors over the requests they consider a bother? The errant clerk should have simply asked for help and completed the assignment with a call to the customer, instead of hoping the issue would go away if she ignored it.

## Know your products

When our office photo copier malfunctioned, the retailer we purchased it from suggested a place we could contact for a technician. The technicians showed up at our office and connected their laptop to our copier. When I asked the technicians to explain the cause of the problem, how they planned to solve it as well as how we could prevent it from recurring, they simply continued with their task. Not until I informed them that they would not be paid for their work unless they answered my questions, did they stop to listen. Then I repeated my questions, but all the technicians could tell me was that the system software had been corrupted and needed to be re-loaded. They did not know how it happened or how to prevent it from happening again.

When I asked for some kind of guarantee to show they believed in their service, they said none was available. I had to labour to explain the assurance a client derives from a guarantee before they finally offered first a three month and then a six month guarantee. Even though they did rectify the problem we had, the technicians were unable to explain why or how it happened, or how to prevent it; which is probably why they started out by ignoring my questions. Ensure that your personnel believe in the product or service you provide and can ably respond to customer questions.

## Listen & communicate clearly

One slip-up is pardonable, but a series, by the same person, on the same evening? Barbara an American, met a friend at a Kampala three star restaurant. They ordered tea and Barbara took great pains to ensure that the waitress understood what herbal tea was. Barbara also ordered tonic water. Ten minutes later, both guests were served very strong, black tea. When asked where Barbara's herbal tea was, the waitress responded "It is finished." Needless to say, Barbara did not drink the tea and did not pay for it. And yes, the tonic water had been forgotten. While ordering her main course, Barbara's guest emphasized that there should be no salad on her plate, but her meal was served with the salad literally spilling off the plate. "I'm sorry madam," was the waitress' flustered response as she took the plate back. Finally, when the waitress brought the bill, it showed a printed total with three decimal places and a hand written total that was double the printed amount, but without decimals. Having lost confidence in the waitress, the dining guests asked a supervisor what the figures meant. Apparently, the printed number was in US dollars and the larger handwritten amount was the Uganda shilling equivalent.

A waitress who appeared to simply not hear some of the guests' requests and a cryptic bill thereafter are reason enough for guests not to want to return to that location. The waitress ought to have written the guests' requests down and come to inform them if any of them could not be fulfilled. Secondly, that restaurant really ought to find a way to insert dollar signs on their bills so customers do not have to decipher the bill once it is presented to them. What measures has your company taken to ensure that the service provided is exactly what the customer asked for?

## Pay attention all the time

One of my friends says the waiters at his health club have become accustomed to chasing after him. When he gets tired of waiting for his bill (and this happens every time he is at the club) he simply gets up and heads for his car. Many a customer opt not to have that second drink, not to order that extra dish or to skip dessert because in addition to being disappointed by incredibly slow service, they also happen to be running out of time. A negligent wait staff leaves customers feeling ignored, irritated, unwilling to tip and sometimes, unwilling to return.

The inattentive attitude of attendants costs the businesses they work for untold lost sales. For waiters and waitresses, it translates into countless missed tips that could go a long way in supplementing their low salaries.

## Do what you are paid for

As part of her application for a South African Study Permit, Joy had to obtain a Certificate of Good Conduct from a police station. On the collection date indicated on her receipt, Joy headed to her local police station, greeted Officer One, informed her why she was there and handed over her receipt. After glancing at the receipt, Officer One looked through a stack of certificates on her desk, told Joy that her certificate was not ready and asked if Joy was sure she had come on the right day. Pointing to the receipt, Joy confirmed that she indeed had the day right. Officer One gave a high pitched laugh, shook her head and declared that Joy's certificate could not possibly be ready because the signing officer had been absent the day before. If Joy was lucky, her document might be ready at 2:00pm. Officer One then walked away.

Enter Officer Two. After hearing Joy's story, Officer Two pulled a stack of papers out of a drawer and asked one of the other officers in the room to call out the names thereon, while he settled down with the day's newspapers. Joy's name was not read out and Officer Two continued to admire the pictures in his newspapers while Joy waited patiently. Almost an hour later, a third officer walked in and upon hearing Joy's predicament, walked her to an office where Officer One was deep in conversation with the signing officer. Obviously, Joy had been forgotten. Following strong encouragement from Officer Three who appeared to be the most senior ranking officer in the room, Joy's certificate was traced in less than 15 minutes.

# JUST DO YOUR JOB

*Listen and communicate clearly*

Clearly, the police officers were more interested in catching up on their social lives than in doing their jobs. If the third officer had not come to Joy's rescue there is no telling how long she might have had to wait for service. Service providers ought to respect their customers' time and respond expeditiously to requests. What delaying tactics do your employees use to put off serving customers as long as they possibly can? Supervisors ought to bring those games to a halt as soon as they begin.

## Sell to interested customers

Jackie ran out of cooking gas at 11.00am one morning so she made what she thought would be a quick trip to the neighbourhood Shell petrol station with an empty Shell gas cylinder in her car. Four hours and several Shell petrol stations later, Jackie still had an empty gas cylinder. On a whim, she decided to try a competitor's petrol station and found it well stocked with gas. The attendant informed Jackie that they had gas but she was "not allowed to buy it with a Shell cylinder." When Jackie offered to purchase both a cylinder and gas from the attendant, he informed her that she was "not allowed" to buy gas from that petrol station without her own gas cylinder. What? Exactly how does the competitor expect anyone to acquire their brand of gas cylinders unless they buy them? This was a very simple request that would have increased that company's gas distribution but they let it go by. Logically speaking, there was no reason to deny Jackie's request to purchase a cylinder with gas. After all, she would have paid for both items. Instead of selling a cylinder and gas to an interested and motivated customer like he was hired to do, the attendant missed an opportunity to make a sale. Train your employees to get customers to spend money in your establishment as opposed to chasing willing spenders away.

## Price accordingly

Do your customers get their money's worth? One November, lured by a fashion studio's radio advertisements, Justine finally decided to sample their tailoring. Justine trustingly dropped off two sets of material, selected two designs off the studio's racks and had her measurements taken. Looking forward to the promised two week turnaround and expecting top notch service for the studio's unit price of US$65, Justine happily parted with a 50 per cent deposit for her Christmas outfits. On the appointed day however, only one of the outfits was almost ready. The second was still just a piece of fabric. Justine finally collected outfit one on Christmas Eve. In January, with no calls from the studio about her second outfit, Justine dropped in. The tailors had apparently forgotten Justine's selected design and created their own. In response to Justine's ensuing tantrum, a tailor took Justine's measurements again, promised to correct the design and call when the dress was ready. In May, with no calls from the studio, Justine made visit four. The lining on her second odd-looking Christmas outfit was visibly hanging beneath the hem so the tailor invited Justine to return later. Wanting only to end her expensive ordeal, Justine opted to wait as the tailor attempted a rescue. Upon getting home, Justine discovered missing buttons on the outfit's back.

The quality of both the fashion studio's tailoring and customer service were substantially below the expectations set by their high prices. Do what your customers expect you to do and be honest with yourself in deciding what price you will charge. Do not charge five star prices for one star work.

## Pay keen attention to customers

Attentive waiters and waitresses are a visible asset in several ways. When Maggie and I had dinner at her favourite neighbourhood restaurant in Maple Grove, Minnesota; it was easy to see why Maggie recommends the place to all her friends. In addition to the delicious food and friendly staff, service was delightfully prompt. TJ our attentive waiter made sure that our glasses were never empty and that each used plate was removed within seconds of our being ready for it to go. When TJ brought us our dessert, he asked if we were interested in ordering anything else. All we wanted however was the bill. While clearing away our dessert plates, just to be sure that he was not missing an opportunity to sell us one last item, TJ politely asked if he could bring us coffee or tea. When we declined, he immediately put our bill on the table. What a treat, not having to wait for our bill. TJ processed our payment and returned right away with our receipt. You can be sure that he walked away with a generous tip and that the next time I am in Maggie's neighbourhood I will stop at her favourite restaurant.

Our waiter paid close attention to us all evening and ensured that we got everything we asked for within good time. We were in very high spirits when we left and naturally, we will recommend that restaurant to anyone looking for a place to eat in Maple Grove, Minnesota. How do you motivate your employees to remain alert and fully in tune with customer needs?

## Value the entire customer experience

Do you care about your customers' entire experience with you or just pieces of it? Diana and Lydia (sisters) and five of their children were visiting Uganda from the United Kingdom for a few weeks. Diana and Lydia were on a mission to show their families all the different Ugandan towns that their mothers lived in as children. Mbale is one of those towns so one morning, the group piled into a four wheel drive vehicle and headed for Mbale. At the first stop, where they had hoped to have lunch, they pulled up to the cold stares of the group of employees standing by the hotel entrance. This frozen welcome prevented the eager travellers from even getting out of their car. Instead, Diana drove to the next hotel where their experience was exactly the opposite. A smiling waiter welcomed them to the hotel's restaurant where for the first time since their Uganda trip had begun, everything on the restaurant menu was actually available. The waiter even knew enough about the menu to answer every question the travellers had and to make suggestions about what each member of the group would enjoy. In addition, the food was excellent.

The entire experience, from start to finish was an enjoyable one, capped off by the waiter regaling the children with local folk tales whenever he stopped by to see how the meal was going. Train your staff to attach value and importance to the entire customer experience, even when it seems an interaction is trivial.

## Make delighting customers your norm
What impression do you have of large government institutions that are supposed to offer services to the public? Slow on delivery, right? Sally recently emigrated from Uganda to the United States. With no plans of ever returning to Uganda, Sally decided to claim her full National Social Security Fund (NSSF) entitlement, including interest. Contrary to the lengthy amount of processing time she imagined such a request would take, the entire exercise from document submission to receipt of funds took just under one month. The Customer Service Officer handling Sally's request not only sent her weekly e-mail updates, but also took the trouble to follow up with NSSF internal audit personnel (who responded in a timely manner) when Sally sent an e-mail asking if she could submit alternative proof documents supporting her claim.

The two officers in two different departments offered Sally helpful and quick service which points to the value the NSSF places on delighting its customers. Do your customers receive consistent treatment from everyone they interact with in your establishment? Or have each of your employees come up with their own personal definition of what customer service ought to be? Make it a point to train all your employees to a consistent level of customer service, providing a uniformly positive experience.

## Offer hassle-free services
A friend recently challenged me to sample the consistently good valet parking services offered by a new parking lot service next to her favourite mall. When you arrive at the lot, a uniformed attendant guides you into any available parking space. You then leave your car keys at the office by the gate and receive a parking ticket bearing your car's license plate number and your arrival time. A uniformed attendant labels your car keys with a tag listing your number plate and hangs the keys on a notice board. When you are ready to leave, you hand in your parking ticket and pay for the service while a uniformed valet positions your car at the

exit, eliminating the hassle of you having to snake your way through the intricate maze of parked cars. Parking for an hour costs US$1.00 but if you have a receipt proving you purchased an item in the mall, you only pay US$0.25.

Kudos are due to the parking service company for meeting a clear need in a congested city by providing professional, hassle-free parking for the patrons of the mall and its environs. The best part of the experience is that it is hassle-free and the attendants are courteous and efficient. Would you use the words hassle-free to describe your customers' experiences with you?

## Points to Ponder

1. Do you have the right people in the right positions in your business? Are the employees who deal with customers suited for the part and do they have the necessary training?

2. What are you going to do about the unqualified relative you hired who is actually a drain on employee morale and performance levels?

3. Have you created performance standards for each position and does every employee know what is expected of them in their job as well as what it means to go the extra mile?

4. What are the consequences for an employee who repeatedly does not meet the required performance standards?

5. How do you reward employees who show the greatest improvement in their on-the-job performance?

6. How do you motivate strong performers to remain with your company and continue delivering excellent results?

## To Do List

- This week, hold one-to-one meetings with your team members. During the meetings, ask them to grade themselves on how well they are doing their job, on a scale of 1 to 5, with 5 being the best performance. Then find out why the individuals assigned themselves that grade. Do you agree with the grade or not? Tell each team member why and ask them how they play to improve their performance.

- Set aside some time to provide on-the-job supervised training for your newest recruits or the team members who seem to be performing below your expectations.

## How Are You Doing?

If a principle is one that you currently practice, put a tick (√) in the Yes column. If a principle is one you need to work on, put a tick in the No column.

| Just Do Your Job | Yes | No |
|---|---|---|
| Display professional conduct | | |
| Follow through to the end | | |
| Be diligent | | |
| Know your products | | |
| Listen and communicate clearly | | |
| Pay attention all the time | | |
| Do what you are paid for | | |
| Sell to interested customers | | |
| Price accordingly | | |
| Pay keen attention to customers | | |
| Value the entire customer experience | | |
| Make delighting customers your norm | | |
| Offer hassle-free services | | |

## CHAPTER 6
## DELIVER WITH SPEED

Nobody likes having to wait. Time cannot be redeemed, once spent. The more service providers come to realize this, the more effort they ought to put into doing whatever they can to save their customers some time. In order to keep our customers, we need to get check-out cashiers to work faster, train bank tellers to process transactions faster, get waiters and waitresses to serve much faster, and get customer service representatives to ignore the numerous personal calls that interfere with customer transactions. Whatever your line of business, how might you serve your customers with increased efficiency?

What can you do to prepare customers for the wait ahead of them? It is standard procedure for airlines to announce the duration of the flight at the beginning of the flight. In some countries, when you call a customer service phone number, within the first few seconds of the call, you learn how many people are ahead of you in the queue and how long of a wait you can expect. You then have the option to remain on hold or request a call back when your phone number gets to the front of the queue. In a rural restaurant I once visited, I was amazed when the waitress who took my lunch order informed me that she would have my plate out in fifteen minutes! These are all efforts to manage peoples' expectations and to let the customer know the amount of time they can plan to dedicate to the activity at hand.

Have you conducted a simple time study on the processes conducted in your business? How long should it take a cashier to ring up a customer who has less than ten items in their shopping basket? How long should customers wait before a waiter or waitress comes to take their order? How long should a customer who calls in have to wait before their call is answered? How fast does your company respond to inquiries made by text message? How long should it take a customer to make a deposit at the teller's window? When an employee falls behind the allocated time for an activity, what back-up plans do you have? At what point do you open another teller's window or another check-out lane? What about creating a "fast lane"? Who would qualify to use it: the elderly, the physically challenged, expectant mothers or shoppers with less than two items? You decide.

If you have not done this yet, commit to putting time aside in order to document the current speeds at which your employees conduct critical customer interfacing tasks. The only tool you will need is a stop-watch. What are current completion times for each task and how would you like them to improve? How much can they realistically improve? Create and distribute a performance standard, which is just a fancy term for a list (see sample below); that dictates the amount of time an employee is supposed to spend on each task that involves customers.

**Table III: Example of estimated task durations**

| | TASK | MAXIMUM DURATION |
|---|---|---|
| 1 | Time customer waits between sitting at table and giving drink order | 2 minutes |
| 2 | Time customer waits to receive drink after placing order | 5 minutes |
| 3 | Time customer waits between placing food order and serving of food | 15 minutes |
| 4 | Time customer waits between finishing meal and receiving receipt | 3 minutes |
| 5 | Time customer waits between paying bill and getting change back | 5 minutes |

Alternatively use the number of customers in any given queue to guide you on when corrective measures need to be taken in the form of sending more staff to the floor. Remember to recognize and reward the employees who are able to deliver within the defined time frames. Your customers will appreciate whatever you do to save their valuable time and they will tell their friends about it.

## Be quick

One Father's Day I was in Maple Grove, Minnesota, USA where I joined some American friends at a neighbourhood restaurant to celebrate the fathers among us. When we entered the restaurant, a waiter put our names on the waiting list and informed us that we would have to wait 15 minutes for a table. Since it was a nice day, we opted to wait outside. 25 minutes later, we were still waiting so one of us went back into the restaurant to find out what was going on. "Another 15 minutes," was the response.

My American friends seemed fine with the news. I kept quiet too but on the inside I was screaming, "It was a 15 minute wait 25 minutes ago!" Ten minutes later our table was ready. After we sat down however, it was another 30 minutes before our meal was served. Although the delicious food was served by a smiling waitress, all I could think of was how painfully slow the process had been and how closely it matched the speed of service in several places in Uganda. False promises, painfully slow service and the absence of any kind of apology thereafter, only lower customer opinions of your establishment. A simple verbal recognition of the inconvenience caused would have transformed this negative experience into a positive one.

## Set high performance standards

Do you set high performance standards irrespective of your competition? As I understand it, in Kampala direct satellite television subscribers can usually obtain a service installation technician within 24 to 48 hours of submitting a request for one. Maggie recently moved from one

US city to another and needed to install DirectTV in her new home. A month before moving, Maggie called DirectTV and obtained an installation date. When the technician arrived on the scheduled day, he was three hours late and claimed he required a letter from the Homeowners' Association authorizing dish installation. Surely, this should have come up when Maggie called to schedule the appointment. Authorization letter in hand, Maggie contacted DirectTV for yet another appointment, only to learn that nothing was available for two weeks. Undeterred, Maggie searched for a local, approved DirectTV retailer who installed her service the very next day. For some additional customer aggravation, Maggie was then required to call DirectTV and inform them that the job had been completed.

Unfortunately, Maggie was stuck with DirectTV's unsatisfactory options and poor customer service just because the competition does not offer as many channels as DirectTV. The minute that scenario changes however, Maggie will switch. Any customer who feels taken for granted is sure to leave the minute a more suitable competitor comes along.

## Run efficient operations

Do you value efficient customer service? Because my bank offers online banking to just a select few, most of the bank's customers have to physically go to the bank for every single bank transaction. On one of my bank trips, there were only three people in line ahead of me. Since there were two tellers on duty, I happily congratulated myself for picking the perfect time for a quick bank stop. To my disappointment however, it took me 40 minutes to reach the teller's window. During that time, the number of customers in line behind me steadily grew. After completing my teller transactions, I asked a customer service representative if I could get a printed statement. The representative showed me to the branch manager's desk where an employee I had never seen before was on the telephone with a bank customer. I sat by that desk for exactly twelve minutes, listening to the ongoing telephone conversation and receiving no acknowledgement of my presence whatsoever, not even a nod or a smile. As I sat there enduring yet another wait, I could not help but think of the amount of time online banking would save both customers and the bank. A bank that extends online banking to just a few really should be more efficient at serving the customers who have no choice but to flock to its banking halls.

Is your business content with slow moving lines served by inefficient staff? Are your employees comfortable taking long personal calls while on duty? Make it your mission to save your customers some time. Assign a staff member to ensure that customer lines keep moving. Better still, include efficient service as an employee performance objective that gets evaluated during employee performance appraisals.

## Demonstrate a sense of urgency

Do you attach value to the demonstration of a sense of urgency? After spending a few days in Uganda, with most of her time at a high-end hotel, an American tourist observed that things in Uganda do not seem to move as fast as they do in Kenya. Needing to have her dress pressed in time for dinner, Aisha called Housekeeping with her request. 30 minutes later, tired of waiting, she ventured into the corridor to see if she could find someone to accelerate a response. Upon opening her door, she saw a solitary uniformed lady dawdling towards her. "Excuse me," Aisha called, "Are you coming to pick up my dress?" The response was "Yes Madam," accompanied by a characteristically Ugandan disarming smile; like the smile would compensate for lost time. No apology for the delay and not even the slightest quickening of the housekeeper's leisurely pace. Fortunately, the dress was eventually pressed to Aisha's satisfaction.

30 minutes was far too long for our international guest (or anyone) to have to wait and the housekeeper who finally showed up acted like she was on holiday, oblivious to the urgency behind the guest's request. The person in Housekeeping who initially took the call ought to have mentioned how long the guest would have to wait for someone to come and pick up her dress. Secondly, the housekeeper ought to have put more pep in her step.

## Delight with speedy delivery

Does your work build or detract from your employer's reputation? Only when I needed to get certified copies of my academic transcript did I realize that I had misplaced the original document. I therefore had to go to my old university, get an original transcript re-issued, make photocopies and have them certified and sealed. Dreading the bureaucracy and unnecessary delays that I expected, I decided to start the process on a Thursday morning. An accommodating officer listened to my request and explained the process. Once I had made the necessary bank payments and returned to him, he escorted me to another room where we submitted a request for my file. To my surprise, my file was retrieved from the archives and delivered to the office where I had begun my mission on the same day. By Tuesday the following week, my transcript had been reissued and I was able to obtain the certified and sealed copies that I needed. Contrary to my pessimistic expectations, the whole exercise took just four working days.

Now, whenever any of my friends bring up the subject of academic transcript retrieval with nothing but negative stories to tell, I am quick to share my personal positive experience. Customers who appreciate the work you do will always come to your defence, should the need arise. They will also pro-actively recommend your company to interested parties.

## Respond as fast as you can

Our office received a call from a lady who claimed she was calling from our national tax authority and wanted to get our company's e-mail address for their database. Believing the caller was part of a scam, I declined to co-operate and told the caller exactly why. The lady on the other side of the line politely replied that she understood my concerns and gave me an official e-mail address that I could contact to verify the call. When I eventually sent the e-mail, I was impressed by the quick and detailed response I received from the authority's Data Take-on Project.

The response came within the hour, thanking me for my query and confirming that the call had indeed been genuine. The e-mail explained that the authority was updating tax payer information in preparation for Kampala Central's transition to electronic services, when the authority would begin communicating with tax payers via SMS and e-mail. Tax payers would therefore get new Tax Identification Numbers (TINs). Instructions on how to obtain the new TINs were also provided.

Consistently polite and quick responses to tax payers will certainly help position a government agency with a reputation for knowing exactly how to extract its pound of flesh and more, as approachable. A friend as opposed to a foe! How many ways might you use efficiency to build a positive image for your business?

## Exceed expectations

Do your customers have high expectations of you? George, in the United States, needed to conduct three transactions using one of his Uganda bank accounts. Although he was concerned about the bank's ability to implement his instructions satisfactorily, he really had no choice. So after notifying the branch manager to expect his instructions, he asked a relative travelling to Uganda to deliver his instructions and signed cheques. As soon as he received the instructions, the branch manager e-mailed George, acknowledging receipt. Over the next two days, George received two more e-mails; one from Susan, a bank employee, seeking clarification on his requested funds transfer and another from the branch manager providing him some options in relation to his requested Fixed Deposit transaction. A few days later, when George's sister stopped by the bank to collect the transaction receipts, she pointed out a paperwork error which the branch manager apologetically offered to correct right away.

In spite of numerous demands on his time, the branch manager went out of his way to handle George's instructions personally, just like George had requested and turned everything around within just three days. Because so many employees seem to be trying to get away with doing as little as possible, customer expectations in this part of the world tend to be set rather low. Consequently, when you simply do just what you are supposed to do in your position, you catapult your company's reputation with any given customer to a whole new and desirable level. When you do just a little more than expected, the results are even better. Do you have expected turnaround times for customer requests? Who monitors employee performance in this regard and how do employees get recognized for exceeding expectations?

## Impress with efficiency

Does the prospect of having to deal with the police for anything whatsoever conjure up nightmares of unnecessary delays and unrivalled inefficiency? If yes, imagine Ruth's amazement when she went through the following pain-free and efficiently conducted exercise at her local Interpol office. As part of her application for a US visa, Ruth had to obtain a Certificate of Good Conduct from the above office. Upon arrival, Ruth was greeted by a smiling officer who directed her to an office where a friendly and knowledgeable officer explained the process Ruth needed to go through. The officer handed her all the necessary forms, provided a template for the letter she had to write and even offered her pen and paper.

As Ruth sat down to complete her paperwork, she wondered whether her entire afternoon would be wasted in the ever lengthening finger-printing queue forming in one corner of the room. Surprisingly however, by the time she had to line up, the queue was gone. The finger-printing section operates like clockwork: hand in forms, get finger prints taken, wash hands and finally, obtain receipt and certificate collection date. Ruth's entire visit lasted only 15 minutes. To crown it all, her documents were actually ready for collection on the designated date, five days later at an Interpol office in another location.

That Interpol office's unexpected efficiency actually brightened up Ruth's day. She was especially pleased to find she had more time on her hands than she had planned for and could even begin the errands she had scheduled for the next day that very afternoon. What changes can you make in the way you do business, to help your customers redeem some time?

## Find ways to be efficient

One morning at around 3:00am, I was one of the miserable, sleep-deprived departing passengers lining up at the immigration booth at Entebbe International Airport. Accustomed to watching passenger after passenger present incomplete immigration cards to the immigration officers and then proceed to complete the cards right there at the window while the rest of us waited, I had prepared myself for just that. Surprisingly however, that morning the line was moving rather fast.

Once I got close enough to hear the immigration officer's voice, I was thrilled to hear him invite each passenger who handed him an incomplete card to step aside and not return until the card was completely filled out. If only all immigration officers would follow his example. And if only all bank tellers would do the same to customers who fill out their withdrawal or deposit slips only after they get to the teller's window.

The immigration officer found a way to do his job efficiently and shorten the time that fully prepared passengers had to spend in line. As a service provider, think of creative ways to increase the efficiency with which you serve your customers. How might you serve more customers, faster?

## Ease processes

My office subscribes to different telecommunication companies for our various telecommunication needs. Unfortunately, postpaid customers with either of those companies are subjected to an extended time lag between invoice issue dates and actual invoice delivery dates (in our case over 20 days), irrespective of delivery mode - mail or courier. In order for us to pay our bills on time, we finally resorted to collecting our invoices in person, soon after the date of issue. Under normal circumstances, should the vendor not do everything in their power to ensure that clients are billed in a timely fashion? Eventually, one of the companies invited us to sign up for electronic invoice delivery. So far, we are pleased with the results.

For providing prompt electronic invoice delivery in a user friendly format at the beginning of each month and thus, eliminating the need for us to pick up our monthly invoice, we are greatly appreciative. How

DELIVER WITH SPEED

*Offer speed*

might you make it easier for customers to do business with you? What unnecessary steps might be eliminated from any given process? If a bank customer fills in their bank account number on a withdrawal slip, must they really fill in their bank branch, which is clearly indicated in the bank account's first three numbers? Eliminate redundancies.

## Points to Ponder

1. How does your personal behaviour in the work place demonstrate the value you attach to efficiency and speed of delivery?

2. Have you created performance standards that dictate the amount of time each task involving customers should take?

3. How might you manage your customers' expectations in relation to time? Ask your team to make suggestions.

4. How can you increase your efficiency of delivery and thus exceed customer expectations?

5. How will you reward the team member who comes up with a way to lower the time spent on any given customer task, by the largest amount of time?

6. Have you any idea how long it takes your competition to handle the same customer related tasks? If not, pay them a visit, with a stop watch in your pocket and time them.

## To Do List

- List the different tasks that require your team to interact directly with customers as well as the amount of time it takes to complete them. Now rank the tasks, with the one that takes the most time at the top and the task that takes the least amount of time at the bottom.

- Ask your team to suggest as many different ways as they can think of to lower the amount of time spent on the two most time consuming customer interactions above.

## How Are You Doing?

If a principle is one that you currently practice, put a tick (√) in the Yes column. If a principle is one you need to work on, put a tick in the No column.

| **Deliver With Speed** | Yes | No |
|---|---|---|
| Be quick | | |
| Set high performance standards | | |
| Run efficient operations | | |
| Demonstrate a sense of urgency | | |
| Delight with speedy delivery | | |
| Respond as fast as you can | | |
| Exceed expectations | | |
| Impress with efficiency | | |
| Find ways to be efficient | | |
| Ease processes | | |

# CHAPTER 7
## COMMUNICATE

When something that impacts your expectations either positively or negatively happens, you would like to be informed. Preferably, this information should reach you well before you actually have to go out and look for it or before you are actually affected by the change. In a similar fashion, your customers would like to be pro-actively informed of any changes that will alter the expectations they have of you and the services or products they obtain from you. In a part of the world where for whatever reason, communication does not come easy, service providers who communicate with their customer base certainly separate themselves from the pack.

Treat your customers like the individuals they are and talk to them. Find out what they are interested in and tell them about the new products or services that you think they might enjoy. Pro-actively inform them about changes that affect them, instead of waiting for them to reach out to you, looking for explanations. When you promise to call, do. If you do not plan to make the call, then simply do not make the promise that you will. Today, we have so many cost-effective means of staying in touch, that businesses really have no excuse. We can communicate in person, on the telephone, via text messages, by e-mail and for the more internet savvy, by using a variety of social networking sites.

Naturally, you will need to have your customers' contact information in order to reach them between physical interactions. Find creative ways to obtain this. For instance, ask customers to fill out a registration form, invite them to sign up for regular updates from your company or to participate in a promotion your company is running. Have a sound reason for asking unregistered customers to leave you their name, telephone number and probably their e-mail address too.

Interestingly enough, the only communications I receive from my mobile telephone company other than my monthly bill, even though I am a long-standing post-paid customer and therefore one of their most reliable and valuable customers, is a nameless text message on the very rare occasions that my bill is past due. That amounts to two text messages in the last seven years. Otherwise, I am completely invisible to them, just an account number in the system. It goes to show that you are not alone in not reaching out to your customers. Even companies in the business of communication find communicating with their customers to be a challenging undertaking.

Fortunately for customers however, that is not true of every business. In Uganda for example, Broadband, an Internet Service Provider is committed to sending text messages to all its current and former customers whenever the network goes down and whenever it is back up and running again. This pre-empts disappointed customer calls from flooding their customer service lines. By keeping their customers informed, they are also lowering the cost of their toll-free customer service number. Some of Uganda's monopolies go a step further and send their customers tailored payment-due reminders by text message. The text messages include the customer's name, number and amount due. This is all done in a timely manner and in a format and language that the customer understands.

Customers will appreciate receiving information from you, even when the news is not good news! Stand out by getting information to your customers well before they ask for it. Even a call, text message or e-mail just to say thank you for being our valued customer will be positively received. Stay in touch.

Since communication is a two-way activity however, in addition to telling your customers what is going on, go ahead and listen. If you need clarification, go ahead and ask, instead of jumping to your own conclusions. Listen and respond to their queries, listen to their comments, listen to their complaints and listen to their feedback. It will be good for you and good for your business.

## Keep customers informed

Over the years, each time Gordon's 10 year old Sony TV has malfunctioned, a neighbourhood electrician has fixed it. Yet another power surge rendered Gordon's TV useless, so he went in search of his seasoned electrician only to find that he was unavailable. The electrician's colleagues therefore referred Gordon to a very young looking Derrick. After Derrick had worked on the TV and walked off with US$15, the picture quality was a far cry from what it used to be and the image on the screen kept changing in size, with each power fluctuation. Gordon endured this for two weeks before the TV finally blew up. Gordon therefore summoned Derrick, who collected the TV and promised to be in touch soon. A week of unanswered and unreturned phone calls followed, with Derrick even switching off his phone whenever Gordon called for updates. Completely frustrated, Gordon made his way to Derrick's repair shop, with the intention of sitting in the shop until Derrick showed up. Claiming that they too were tired of Derrick's poor customer support and obstinate attitude, his coworkers summoned him to the repair shop. Upon arrival, Derrick proceeded to narrate a very tall tale which Gordon might have appreciated if only Derrick had bothered to answer or return his numerous calls earlier on.

Avoiding Gordon's calls and not providing any updates far outweighed Derrick's inability to fix Gordon's TV. You will find that customers are more amenable when you pro-actively provide them with updates, irrespective of whether they are good or bad. A good way to lose a customer, however, is to wait until they contact you, only to hear nothing but bad news.

## Build Trust

An administrative assistant called a telephone service provider about installing voice-mail on their office land lines. The customer service representative who spoke to the assistant assured her that the phone company was working on a few things and soon, voice-mail would be available for everyone who requested it. The representative then requested the assistant to call back in three months. For a year after that call, the assistant called the phone company every three months and each time, the conversation was exactly the same. The customer service representative would offer to check with someone else, put the assistant on hold and return to the call a few minutes later, only to invite the assistant to call back again in another three months. After a year-long wait for voice-mail, the assistant finally recommended that the company invest in an antiquated answering machine instead.

Customer service should make sure it has up to date information on the availability of company products and should be proactive about following up with customers to provide updates, as opposed to waiting for customers to contact them, only to hear the same long story each time.

## Inform customers of changes

The local aviation authority that oversees one of our international airports recently made some interesting changes. The road leading to the passenger departure level in the main terminal was blocked without notice. Travellers who were unaware of this development discovered upon arrival at the airport, that vehicles had to be parked in the public parking yard on a lower level and that they had to find a way of getting themselves and their luggage to the departure level. Clearly, visible signs pointing out the newly restricted areas, the resulting detours and suggesting that travellers obtain a luggage trolley, if they needed one would have been much appreciated. However, no such signs were installed. Indeed, on two separate occasions, I watched departing travellers lug heavy luggage in the direction they thought they should go, only to find they were heading the wrong way. They then had to retrace their steps back to the parking yard where they asked for directions to the upper level.

Abandoning airport users to their own devices in navigating through changes at the airport is no way to do business. I am no airport administration expert but by simply thinking in business terms, I have no doubt that the aviation authority should have been responsible for making sure that appropriately placed signs informed the public of the changes as well as where to go.

## Communicate requirements up front

My Malawi-based friend Joy attends university in a Southern African country which requires her to have a study permit. In Malawi, that country's High Commission processes study permits on the same day. Joy's study permit expired while she was in Kampala however, so she decided to renew it at that country's Kampala High Commission. Unfortunately, the visa officer she spoke to would not accept her application without a Malawi Police Clearance. Overhearing the exchange a supervisor intervened, telling Joy that they could obtain the required clearance from the Malawi High Commission. Joy should therefore return the next day for an interview. When Joy returned, she was again asked to submit a current Malawi Police Clearance. So Joy had to leave yet again and think of a creative way of getting the document she had been asked for.

Fortunately, a friend in Malawi was able to quickly process the clearance and immediately e-mailed it to Joy. Clearance in hand, Joy made trip three to the High Commission and asked when her permit would be ready since she had until midday to change her air ticket. In response, the visa officer kindly offered to call "before afternoon" with Joy's permit status.

The call however, did not come so Joy reluctantly spent $50 to postpone her flight. Joy then called the High Commission and learned that her passport would be ready that afternoon at 2:00pm. Had she been informed by midday as promised, she would not have had to postpone her flight.

By making all requirements known at the beginning of a process and by simply picking up the telephone and making promised update calls, service providers can save customers a lot of time, money and unnecessary turmoil.

## Call your customers

For some reason, service providers in this part of the world tend not to call their customers, ever. In my perpetual search for a hairdresser who

COMMUNICATE

cares about more than just getting my money, I scheduled an appointment with yet another one. Imagine how pleasantly surprised I was when at 7:30am on the morning of my appointment, the new hairdresser called me. She wanted to find out if she could move my appointment to 12:30pm from 10:30am. I was incredibly pleased that she had bothered to call and check with me, giving me an opportunity to re-arrange my schedule too.

How many times have you wished that a service provider had called to inform you about a new product, to reschedule an appointment or even just to ask when they can expect to see you again? With all the attractive deals the phone companies are handing out these days, surely service providers can afford to make some calls. It makes a world of difference. Customers will be pleased to know that you think about them and if your action saves your customers some time and money, they will be all the happier.

## Notify customers in good time
Instead of keeping my hard earned money within easy reach under my pillow, I choose to deposit it in a bank with the understanding that when I need to withdraw some, all I have to do is walk into my branch during working hours and claim what belongs to me. I bank at my chosen branch location for the lighter traffic, shorter customer lines and ample parking space. Now, every once in a while the bank's system "hangs up." Sometimes the problem is bank-wide. At other times, only a single branch is affected for days on end.

When I walked into the banking hall that Tuesday morning, it was not until I reached the teller's window that I learned the system was down and all withdrawals suspended. Whenever this happens, the tellers happily invite disappointed customers to try other bank branches - locations we avoid for reasons already mentioned.

Instead, my bank should consider borrowing a leaf from one of our internet service providers and proactively notify customers whenever the system is down. Waiting until time-strapped customers are at the teller's window before informing them that their funds are inaccessible is simply not the way to go. Customers waste too much irredeemable time that way and are never happy about it.

## Communicate even the bad news

Do you ever wish for more airline options? Early one morning Geoffrey drove his son Vernon to Entebbe International Airport. A group from Vernon's school was booked on a 5:10am flight to Nairobi, en-route to Dakar, Senegal. Geoffrey arrived at the airport at 3:45am but Aviation Security barred Vernon from reaching the check-in area upon instructions from the airline. Afraid Vernon would miss his flight, Geoffrey insisted on obtaining an explanation. An airline employee eventually sauntered out at 4:10am to inform the growing group that the counter had closed at 4:00am because the flight was overbooked. Following a colourful verbal exchange, Vernon boarded the "overbooked" flight, only to find several empty seats on board.

That Sunday in Dakar, Vernon's group checked in for the flight home. An hour after scheduled departure time, passengers learned their flight would leave 24 hours later. Non-Senegalese passengers were bussed to hotels, forced to share rooms and given no means of contacting the people awaiting their return. 24 hours later, the flight left Dakar an hour late. In Nairobi on Tuesday morning, Vernon's tired group boarded the 7:55am to Entebbe at 9:00am.

The airline offered no explanations. After another 30 minute luggage-loading delay, the flight departed. Finally, Vernon's incredibly exhausted group landed in Entebbe late Tuesday morning, to the immense relief of several flustered and weary parents.

By simply being polite, communicating exactly what was going on, apologizing for the delays and offering passengers a means of getting in touch with their families, the airline would have successfully managed its passengers' growing frustration.

## Explain when customers ask

I went to my bank to send a Real Time Gross Settlement (RTGS). For faster service, although I am not a paid-up member of the preferred customer club, I went to the preferred customer counter. Just like she does every time I do this, the teller's greeting was: "We will charge you US$10." Wishing she would smile, just once, I replied "That's fine." The teller looked at my RTGS form and asked me for a cheque. This puzzled

COMMUNICATE

*Provide information*

me because I had not had to attach accompanying documents before. I therefore challenged the teller who then referred me to her supervisor.

I explained to the supervisor that because I had not had to attach a cheque before, I had not even brought my cheque book with me. Could he tell me why and when this had become a requirement, as well as why it had not been communicated? The gentleman's response: "That's the way it is now." He went on to suggest that I could either go and get a cheque or ask someone to bring one in on Monday. In response to my request for an immediate solution, he offered a US$10 counter cheque. Frustrated, I left the bank without completing my transaction. A few phone calls revealed that banks were adopting the cheque requirement as an anti-fraud measure.

I wonder why the bank employees I spoke to did not explain this to me. A simple explanation will put customers in a much better frame of mind.

## Bill with care

I just got yet another threatening sms from my mobile phone service provider, informing me that my bill was past due and that my number would soon be disconnected. Given that I always go to great lengths to personally pick up my monthly invoices from the provider and pay them on time, I had finally had enough. I therefore gave "Elizabeth" (the name at the end of the threatening sms), a call.

To cut a very long story short, it turns out that on some invoices, the "invoice amount" differs from the "amount due". In my case, on one of my invoices, the amount due (which is the amount I always pay) was lower than the invoice amount. Although subsequent invoices showed that I was up to date on my bill payments, Elizabeth's master statement (which does not get sent to customers) tracks the difference between what you pay and what you owe. In other words, unbeknown to me, I am on Elizabeth's black list due to an internal invoice discrepancy that I would never have discovered had I not called.

Not synchronizing records so that everyone is on the same page is nothing short of careless. All companies ought to exercise extreme care when billing and customers need to carefully scrutinize all bills.

COMMUNICATE

*Offer helpful responses*

## Always follow-up

When our ICT support company recommended that we try a new internet service provider's five day internet trial, we quickly agreed. A sales lady representing the new entrant came to the office and signed us up. A few days later, the provider's contractors installed a mast on our building and configured our computers. The following morning, however, we were unable to connect to the internet.

After our IT support changed the Internet Provider addresses set the day before, we were able to connect, but only intermittently. Calls to customer service yielded the recommendation that we increase our bandwidth, advice which our IT support asked us to ignore.

After that, we called customer service twice more. Both times they promised to send someone to our office to solve the problems we were experiencing. We waited for three weeks and instead, received a text message announcing that our account with the company would be closed unless we paid our dues. What dues and what account?

We signed up for a five day trial and a month later, nobody had bothered to find out if we were satisfied with the trial or to transition us to a proper account. To crown it all, their sales lady boldly delivered an invoice, acknowledged her negligence – she had had personal problems - and apologized. Customers should never have to pay the price for your company's negligence. Additionally, an employee who tells a customer about their personal problems is simply being inappropriate. Besides, most customers are really not interested.

As soon as the five day trial was over, somebody should have checked in with us to find out if we had enjoyed the experience or not. Had we been impressed we would have signed up on the spot. As it was however, we were not impressed and if someone had checked with us, it would have been their duty to find out why and provide our reasons to the responsible party back at their office. Thereafter, the company should have taken appropriate action to eliminate the reason for our discontent.

## Manage expectations through communication

"I'll be there in five minutes," is the confident reply when you ask your special hire taxi driver how soon he thinks he will reach you.

15 minutes later, "I'll be there in five minutes." And you are left wondering whether a minute is always equal to 60 seconds or whether some people have privileged access to minutes with more seconds than yours.

This is why I commend the taxi driver I regularly use. Somehow John came to the realization that if he was to retain this customer, he would always have to keep time. And when he is running late, he always calls me to ask for an additional five, ten or 15 minutes, whatever the case may be. A simple phone call to manage customer expectations - very high returns. That is winning service!

## Build rapport through communication

I stumbled upon a new hair salon in my neighbourhood. Given the complete lack of effort to cultivate customer loyalty on the part of my hairdresser at the time, visiting the new hair salon and subsequently switching were very easy decisions for me.

Irene my new hairdresser is a consummate professional who has set very high standards for her services and for the large, uncluttered, airy and clean hair salon in which she operates.

In sharp contrast to other hairdressers I have been to, Irene discusses everything she plans to do to my hair with me, as well as the products she plans to use and their expected effect.

Furthermore, Irene is committed to continuous improvement and actually invites and implements customer suggestions on how she might serve them better. Together, we have experimented with new hair products and collaboratively found new ways to handle my hair. I feel like her partner, not just a source of revenue. Irene is a winner for maintaining dialogue with her clientele and for striving to retain loyal, repeat customers. How do you treat your customers?

Have you ever taken the time to find out how they feel about the services you offer? They just might have some valuable suggestions for you. Remember that customers who feel like they are worth more to you than just their money are more likely to keep returning.

## Points to Ponder

1. What are you going to do to let your customers know about the new stock you just received, the new product you are about to introduce or the promotional sale you are about to hold?

2. What do you do when you cannot deliver an order to a customer on time?

3. When you are running behind your appointment schedule, what do you do to inform the customers who are on your appointment schedule that you are running late?

4. How have you equipped your staff to professionally and effectively handle customer queries about your products? What kind of in-house training do your employees need in order for them to ably respond to customers?

5. How do you follow-up with customers who are using your products on a trial basis?

6. What new ideas for your business have you come across during conversations with your customers?

COMMUNICATE

## To Do List

⊙ Find out how much it will cost you to send a text message to your entire customer list or database. Now go on and send your customers a message – season's greetings, new products in stock or even just "Thank you for being a valued customer."

⊙ If you offer customers goods on credit, make a list of the customers who owe you money and send them a friendly and polite text message reminder. The message should include the customer's name, the exact amount owed and the payment due date.

## How Are You Doing?

If a principle is one that you currently practice, put a tick (√) in the Yes column. If a principle is one you need to work on, put a tick in the No column.

| Communicate | Yes | No |
|---|---|---|
| Keep customers involved | | |
| Build trust | | |
| Inform customers of changes | | |
| Communicate requirements up front | | |
| Call your customers | | |
| Notify customers in good time | | |
| Communicate even the bad news | | |
| Explain when customers ask | | |
| Bill with care | | |
| Always follow-up | | |
| Manage expectations through communication | | |
| Build rapport through communication | | |

# CHAPTER 8
# OFFER SEAMLESS SERVICE

Customers do not know and in most cases actually do not want to know what you have to do in order to render them the services they pay you for. All we want is the finished product or service we are looking for. Service providers are responsible for seeing to it that the delivery process is seamless and without hitch. Create system checks to ensure that your systems are working to deliver the quality your customers expect and always have a back-up plan in case your system fails, for whatever reason. Internal breakdowns should be invisible to your customers.

Kampala's Nasser Road might as well be called Stationery Avenue. Almost every single shop stocks stationery. When a customer asks for an item that a retailer on this street does not have, the retailer's standard response is "Would you mind waiting for a few minutes while I check in the store?" The retailer then retreats to the shop's rear exit and unbeknown to the customer, literally sprints to the neighbouring shops looking for the requested item until he or she finds it. A few minutes later, the retailer steps back into the front of the shop with a box of the requested item, and the customer is none the wiser. All the customer knows is that they entered a shop and were able to get everything they wanted. That is seamless service. The customer has no need to know – and really is not interested in knowing - what you have to go through to get them what they came to you for. So please spare us the long stories about not having a generator, the waiter who did not show up or even your unpaid monthly salary.

Some companies really give you the impression that they only remain in business because they have no sound competition. There seems to be no connection between the services offered by two different departments within the same company, and when one department fails to deliver, there is no back-up whatsoever!

Instead, find creative ways to offer your customers seamless service, that is, service without hiccoughs. Are you experiencing an electricity outage? Then where is your generator or inverter? Why is there no diesel for the generator? Did your electronic file disappear? Why was the file not backed up? Did you register my complaint two days ago? So how come I have to call back again to make exactly the same complaint to a person with a voice that sounds exactly like the person I spoke to two days ago? You said I could order anything I wanted off the menu so how come the chef feels comfortable enough to send me a message saying he is too busy to prepare individual a la carte requests so I should select something from the buffet? It took you 30 minutes to come and take my order because some of the waiters did not show up for work today – considering that you opened your doors for service, how does that concern me? Nobody in my town has had access to our telephone network in over twelve hours and when I call to find out what is going on, you tell me you were unaware of the problem? What happened to back-up systems that kick in once the main system fails? Need I go on? Take a leaf from the creative book of Kampala's Nasser Road stationery vendors. No matter what it takes, do everything you can to ensure that your customer walks out with what they came in for, within what the customer considers a reasonable time frame.

Beyond seamless service delivery, customers should view the entire business as one. The treatment they receive from the receptionist ought to match the treatment they receive from the shop attendant and from the cashier. It should be consistent. In the same manner, a promise made by your customer service manager, should be upheld by your technical staff. Present yourself as a unified team, operating as one.

## Track customer transactions accurately

Ayub deposited a client payment of US$250 on his bank account. Because it was a cheque from the same bank, he fully expected the funds to be available within 48 hours. Several days later, Ayub returned to his bank branch to make a withdrawal, only to learn that his earlier deposit had not yet been credited. According to customer service, the bank had absolutely no record of Ayub's deposit and since he did not have a deposit slip as proof, nothing could be done.

Baffled that the bank had no record of the transaction, Ayub insisted that the bank call his client for verification. Even a series of several phone calls between the bank, the issuing client and Ayub could not prove his claim. In spite of the client providing an account number, the cheque number and issue date, it actually began to seem like a completely lost cause. Ayub was therefore asked to leave the matter in his bank's "capable" hands but two weeks later, the cheque was still missing. A month after making what had started feeling like an imaginary deposit, Ayub asked his client to cancel the missing cheque and pay him by electronic fund transfer instead. Shortly thereafter, you guessed it -the invisible cheque materialized.

Misplacing a deposited cheque, having no transaction record and absolutely confounding a customer – this should have happened somewhere else, but not at a bank. Every business should have a way of keeping accurate records of all customer transactions and making sure there is a back-up system, even if it is a manual one, just in case the first method fails.

## Streamline internal communications

Does your company have a sound process for handling customer complaints? When my friend Sophie moved to an up-market Kampala suburb, she watched one of the exposed water pipes on her street leak for a full year before calling the national water corporation to report the exposed leaking pipe. Within a few days, the water corporation had buried the pipe.

The company forgot however, to repair the leak before burying the pipe. Thereafter, Sophie drove past a large water puddle in the exact location where the exposed leaking pipe once lay. Now in the company's defence, there is no running water in that neighbourhood during the day. It is conceivable therefore that whoever buried the exposed pipe did not notice the leak and simply buried the pipe. Interestingly however, for over three months thereafter, Sophie received numerous calls from a water company customer service officer asking if her complaint had been resolved; and Sophie continuously informed the caller that the buried pipe was still leaking underground.

Congratulations to the water company for burying the pipe and for the follow-up calls. One wonders however, what the calls are for if the feedback received is ignored. The apparent breakdown of internal communication is a shame. Details from the initial complaint appear to have been misplaced and feedback from the follow-up calls seems not to get forwarded. Service providers ought to make sure that communication between their different departments is well coordinated and streamlined. Otherwise, what is the point of having departments that offer complementary services but do not speak to each other?

## Link internal systems

Are customers driven to extremes just to gain access to your services? My friend Susan had to throw a tantrum to get her internet wireless connection activated. The situation has been so bad for so long that Susan wonders whether one of our mobile phone companies actually has a call centre or merely pretends to have one. Every time Susan replenishes her internet account remotely, she sends an activation text message to the designated number, receives a message back asking her to wait for activation but several hours later, she finds herself calling the company's help lines repeatedly to ask why her connection is still down. Susan asserts that in four years with that mobile phone company she is yet to speak to a real person on the other side of the help line.

The network is always busy. On numerous occasions, she has then had to drive to the company's service centre, which completely nullifies the benefits of remote activation. The explanation the phone company provides is invariably -"The network is down." After loading airtime remotely one Saturday and subsequently making that inconvenient and unfruitful trip to the service centre, by the following Monday morning Susan's connection was still inactive. The result: a second trip to the service centre where this time, Sophia's dramatic tantrum actually resulted in immediate activation.

Should that be what it takes? Why should a company drive a customer into making a scene before she can access the services she has already paid for? Needless to say, Susan is with a different mobile phone company now.

## Stay aware of item availability

A group of my friends were at one of Kampala's hotel restaurants for a long awaited reunion tea. After consulting their waiter, they ordered tea and three servings of a menu item that lists plantains as an ingredient. The waiter placed their order and returned to inform them that it was well underway. Several minutes later, someone who appeared to be a supervisor came to the ladies' table to ask them to change their order because the hotel was out of plantains. Surprised that communication between the kitchen and the wait staff could be that disconnected at that particular hotel of all places, my friends said as much to the apologetic supervisor.

Disappointed, the ladies settled for tilapia fish fillets following the supervisor's confident assurance that fillets were indeed available.

Just as the ladies were resuming their conversation, the supervisor returned with an update - there were no fish fillets in the kitchen. Promising to compensate my friends for the poor service, the supervisor took their third and final order – samosas (meat-filled, triangle shaped pastries). What compensation was offered? Complimentary tea! My friends paid full price for the snacks which had caused their disappointment.

The staff members taking orders overlooked the importance of knowing which menu items were actually available, resulting in a less than satisfactory customer experience. Wait staff ought to be fully aware of what is available in the kitchen at all times. Better still, the kitchen should never run out of items listed on the menu. Similarly, retailers should always make sure their shelves are well-stocked with the products customers come to their shops for. A disappointed customer might choose to start shopping elsewhere.

## Install system checks

What measures do you take to eliminate customer disappointment? Geoffrey, who is a frequent flyer calls one of East Africa's airlines "a disaster just waiting to happen!" According to Geoffrey, a Zimbabwean friend's wife passed away in Kampala so the family arranged to fly the mortal remains back to Harare. The remains began their journey from Entebbe to Harare on a Friday and were expected in Harare later the same day. The anxious, bereaved family was at Harare International Airport at the flight's scheduled arrival time but had to leave the airport empty handed, because their delivery was nowhere to be found. Somebody neglected to off-load the remains in Harare so they travelled on to Lusaka and back to Nairobi. A distraught family finally obtained the body the following day.

Causing a grieving family indescribable anguish by not making the expected delivery in the right place at the right time was simply unacceptable. Unbelievably, the airline did not offer an apology or any form of compensation. Surely an international airline ought to have a system with checks to prevent this kind of thing from happening.

## Fix system glitches swiftly

I rushed into my bank with a number of financial obligations to meet that day. I was surprised to find however, that all activity seemed to be at a standstill. Hoping to shorten my visit, I headed to the preferred customer section where I mistakenly attributed the customers' glum faces to the gloomy weather. When I finally got to the teller, she looked at my cheque and announced that I could not withdraw any money because the system was down. "When do you expect the system to be back up again?" I asked. The teller shrugged, said she could not determine that and flippantly suggested that I try another branch. Realizing that this teller would not be the best source of additional information, I headed to customer service. Apparently the bank had recently installed a "new and improved" system, my branch's server was too slow to handle it and for an entire week, the system had been on and off, sometimes shutting down for over three hours at a time.

How did the bank fall short? Not being able to release funds to depositors on demand for several days, as well as flippant tellers with nonchalant suggestions to frustrated yet loyal customers who expect their chosen branch to meet their needs. Do you have a back-up plan that kicks in when your systems fail? And when systems fail, are you equipped to have them back up and running as soon as possible?

## Prepare contingency plans

Elaine and Rene were visiting Uganda from the US for the first time and opted to spend most of their stay in Jinja at one of Jinja's large hotels. Although the place appeared completely deserted and they felt like the only guests on their first night there, the hotel's visual impact and impressive views more than compensated for Elaine and Rene's feelings of isolation. That evening, the hungry duo went to the empty hotel restaurant for dinner. Twice, they placed their orders and twice, it took the waiter over 20 minutes to return and let them know that the items they had ordered were unavailable. Finally, their 3rd order happened to be something that could be prepared. Fortunately for Elaine and Rene, on their 2nd day in Jinja, the hotel hosted a large residential conference – at last sufficient reason to stock and staff the kitchen. Thanks to the large group, for the rest of their stay the guests were able to get everything they ordered in good time.

The waiter really should have come back much sooner to let the guests know that the items they had ordered were not available. More importantly however, this hotel should have had a plan for efficiently and effectively catering to all paying guests irrespective of their number.

## Provide alternatives

I was in Nairobi working with a group of women entrepreneurs from Ethiopia, Kenya, Tanzania and Uganda, all participants in a three year Women Entrepreneur Development Programme that includes a series of mandatory workshops. The workshop locations rotate among the four countries listed above. The minute the two ladies from Ethiopia learned where I was from, they approached me with their tale of woe they had missed the Uganda workshop a couple of months earlier because they had been denied Uganda visas in Addis Ababa, Ethiopia.

Rachel and Helene had asked the workshop hosts in Kampala to e-mail their workshop invitation letters directly to Uganda's Addis Embassy. The hosts complied, copying each visa applicant. Several days later, with no response from the embassy, Rachel and Helene printed copies of their invitation letters, attached them to their visa applications and submitted them for processing. The officer who received their paperwork and application fees asked them to collect their passports after 4:00pm that afternoon.

When the ladies returned, their visa fees were refunded. Their applications had been denied because their invitation letters were not original documents. Upon learning this, the Kampala hosts called the embassy seeking a means of faxing the letters. The embassy officer who answered the phone curtly informed the caller that the embassy had "no power" and could not receive faxes, then hung up. With e-mails and faxes ruled out, what were the ladies to do, but miss the workshop?

Providing only obstacles and no solutions is no way to endear oneself to customers. The embassy should have a back-up plan that allows visa applicants to submit visa applications even when the embassy has "no power!"

## Provide uninterrupted service

Henry woke up at 2:30am to catch a flight from Entebbe to Nairobi on a regional airline. In Nairobi, Henry's connecting flight to Harare should have left at 8:00am, but finally left at 1:00pm. Why? Officially, the airline was experiencing a "technical problem." Through his informal research however, Henry learned that the airline had recently installed a new electronic roster that apparently kept allocating crews that were still inbound from other locations to flights scheduled for departure. To translate, the crew that had been allocated to Henry's 8:00am Harare flight was on its way from Bombay so, airline staff were busy physically calling and convincing crew members (who should have been resting) to man a flight whose scheduled crew was otherwise occupied.

During Henry's seven hour wait in the airport lounge, he counted a total of six flights that were delayed for four to six hours, for the same reason. I leave the possible consequences of using tired crews to your imagination.

Now surely, an airline ought to have a means of checking and/or overriding any new system and without doubt, ought to have a back-up plan to ensure uninterrupted service.

## Align operations

Does your business depict a consistent story? I was booked on a regional airline from Nairobi to Lusaka, with a scheduled boarding time of 7:05am. At 7:50am, we the waiting passengers patiently watched a uniformed pilot stroll through the boarding area and board our plane. Ten minutes later, an airline employee walked by announcing that we had not yet boarded because of a crew delay. Curious, I asked the airline employee what he meant by "crew delay." The employee's translation - "The pilot was late!" We boarded shortly thereafter and the plane pushed back from the gate at 8:45am, 35 minutes behind schedule. In his apology, the pilot unabashedly blamed the delay on a change of aircraft, which according to him, called for a different pilot than originally assigned.

Changes behind the scenes should be completely invisible to customers. Schedules should be adhered to and companies that are not able to deliver on time should not offer their customers excuses. We all understand that delays happen sometimes and in those cases, companies should pre-empt customer questions and discomfort with proactively given apologies.

## Depict a consistent image

Do you strive to depict a consistently favourable image? I once had the pleasure of travelling to Senegal, courtesy of a client who hosted 50 of

*Provide alternatives*

us at what he called an idyllic location. Initially the beach hotel, about 80 kilometres from Dakar did not disappoint. The ocean side property boasts a sandy beach, double storied structures with simple but comfortable furnishings and a non-English speaking staff who for the most part, wear heart-warming smiles. Our entire group thoroughly enjoyed our first dinner and the accompanying live band. Everything up to that point set our expectations for a delightful time ahead. The next morning however, we experienced an overwhelming deterrent to our enjoyment. All meals were served buffet style and on patrol, alighting on any exposed food at every breakfast and lunch thereafter, was an aggressive swarm of flies irrespective of whether the meal was served indoors or outdoors. Meal times became a juggling act as we all struggled to eat and keep the flies away simultaneously. Fortunately, the flies were off duty at dinner time.

Failing to control the fly traffic at meal times overshadowed everything else and had us all wondering about the hotel's kitchen hygiene. A voluntary return visit is highly unlikely. Take a critical look at your business. Might there be something there, no matter how small, that does not fit with your overall image and simply puts customers off?

## Train all employees to value customers

Do all your employees value your customers? In spite of once finding a cockroach in my veggie burger at a cafe close to my office, I keep going back there. Why? Because the manager on duty that day was profoundly apologetic and immediately offered me a replacement meal; the enthusiastic waitresses more than compensate for the lackadaisical ones and it is only a three minute drive from my office. One Saturday, I stopped at the cafe to see if as promised by some waitresses there, chapatti (fried flatbread) was indeed available on demand even though it is not a menu item. It took my waitress 15 minutes to return to my table and inform me that my order could not be made. It had taken her that long to try and cajole the chef into fulfilling my request. The cafe was deserted that evening so clearly, the chef was not busy. He simply did not feel like making chapattis and no one on duty could overrule his decision. I left, disappointed and determined never to voluntarily return to a place where the chef, not the customer reigns supreme.

Losing a customer because a chef decided the customer's simple request felt like too much work is simply unacceptable. Establishments ought to train all staff members to value customers. Clearly, this chef had missed the class.

## Work as a team

One afternoon, a group of visiting university students stopped for lunch at a small upcountry hotel. When Rebecca came to take their order, everyone wanted something different so Rebecca decided to invite Chef Patrick to the table, so that he could tell the guests exactly what was available. The chef said he was happy to prepare anything for which he had ingredients in stock. He then gave the guests two sets of menu options. Items that required about 15 minutes of preparation time, followed by items that required more than 30 minutes.

Rebecca cleverly reduced what could have turned into several trips between the kitchen and this particular table to just one trip by inviting the chef over. Chef Patrick happily cooperated, treated the guests cordially and accommodated their requests, visibly demonstrating the value he attaches to customers. The team was efficient, courteous and coordinated. Those students will surely return to that hotel the next time they are in that part of the country.

## Infuse all employees with customer service

I once had to spend the night before an early morning flight in a boutique hotel a few kilometres away from our international airport. From the moment a waiter in the garden welcomed me, I knew I was in for a treat. Welcoming staff smiles aside, the small hotel felt very comfortable, was simply yet tastefully furnished and served delicious meals. During my night there, I had to e-mail a client report to meet a deadline but could not get online using the available in-house computer. Without prompting, one of the employees invited me to use the administrative computer which I gratefully did. To my expression of appreciation, his simple response was "You already paid for it!" When I requested a 3:00am wake-up call, the receptionist inquired as to whether I wanted breakfast at the same time. My negative answer resulted in the friendly advice that I at least have coffee or juice because again, I had already paid for it! The next morning, I enjoyed a complimentary ride to my destination (I had already paid for it!) and thankfully, the hotel driver fully cognizant of my preference to observe total silence that early in the morning, made no attempt to engage me in conversation.

A welcoming environment and consistently flawless customer service at every turn set that hotel apart. The atmosphere and every aspect of service worked together to create an unforgettable experience. All your employees should be trained to pay attention to even the smallest of details affecting customers. The returns in the form of customer loyalty and word-of-mouth advertising are well worth the effort.

## Demonstrate high performance standards

For our February Girls' Night Out, someone suggested a newly opened Italian restaurant. I had never been there so I had no idea what to expect. Upon arrival, we were immediately impressed by the restaurant's elegant style; clearly a fine dining establishment. A waiter quickly showed us to our reserved table and took our drink orders. When Tambo realized that most of us had ordered water, instead of cluttering our table with several 500 ml bottles, he showed up with enough 1,500 ml bottles to cater to our needs - a space and cost saving that did not go unnoticed. We then got so engrossed in our conversation that when Tambo returned for our food orders, we were not ready. Our request for a few more minutes was met with a gracious smile; a sharp contrast to the long faces this request is usually met with. When we were finally ready to order, we bombarded Tambo with several questions about the menu. Without having to return to the kitchen to consult, Tambo competently fielded all our inquisitive questions including translations from Italian, details on ingredients and even various methods of food preparation. In our city, this was definitely a first.

# KEEPING CUSTOMERS

*Offer solutions not excuses*

Elegantly appointed surroundings, delicious food, and the biggest surprise of all – friendly, attentive and knowledgeable waiters. We were duly impressed.

## Fulfil your slogan's promise

Although I was determined to keep an open mind as I began my first ever trip to a remote town in the south west of the country, I found myself replaying "helpful" comments from some of my friends – "There is no internet", "You need a four-wheel drive", "A week there is too long!" and this from people who either hail from that part of the country or had recently been there. Imagine my surprise therefore, when an assistant manager at the hotel where I would be staying came to open my car door as soon as our car stopped. That marked the beginning of what turned out to be several days of customer-delighting treatment from every single member of staff, including trainees.

The manager was open to rate negotiations; the waitresses were attentive and open to menu combination changes; one called Dorothy stands out for always telling me how many minutes my orders would take. In contrast to Kampala, used dishes disappeared immediately and seconds later, bills were presented with a smile. Returning to the hotel every evening felt like coming home to a warm family. We could all learn a thing or two about hospitality from that hotel whose slogan is "Hospitality is our passion." Every single employee at the hotel worked to make the hotel slogan a reality.

## Points to Ponder

1. What does your attitude towards customers communicate about how customers should always be treated, by every team member?

2. Do all your team members view and treat customers the same way? Does a single customer service attitude prevail throughout the organization?

3. Does the way your company treats employees support or contradict your company vision, mission and/or tag line? How?

4. How have you equipped your employees to work as a team, with each one supporting the other especially when it comes to handling customers?

5. Do your frontline employees remain aware of available products from the company as a whole, in the store or even in the kitchen, as the case may be? What systems have you devised to keep them informed?

6. Do you have a backup system for all the services you offer and if yes, how effective is it? Have you tested it?

## To Do List

⊙ During your next staff meeting, ask team members how they feel when the person providing them a service offers a long list of excuses for not delivering the expected results. Now ask them to think back to the times when they have done the same thing to your customers. What steps will they now take to improve their performance?

⊙ Hold an in-house brainstorming session where employees suggest different ways to create backup systems to ensure that the customer always gets what they came for, no matter what. Offer a prize for the practical suggestions that you decide to implement.

## How Are You Doing?

If a principle is one that you currently practice, put a tick in the Yes column. If a principle is one you need to work on, put a tick (√) in the No column.

| **Offer Seamless Service** | Yes | No |
|---|---|---|
| Track customer transactions accurately | ☐ | ☐ |
| Streamline internal communications | ☐ | ☐ |
| Link internal systems | ☐ | ☐ |
| Stay aware of item availability | ☐ | ☐ |
| Install system checks | ☐ | ☐ |
| Fix system glitches swiftly | ☐ | ☐ |
| Prepare contingency plans | ☐ | ☐ |
| Provide alternatives | ☐ | ☐ |
| Provide uninterrupted service | ☐ | ☐ |
| Align operations | ☐ | ☐ |
| Depict a consistent image | ☐ | ☐ |
| Train all employees to value customers | ☐ | ☐ |
| Work as a team | ☐ | ☐ |
| Infuse all employees with customer service | ☐ | ☐ |
| Demonstrate high performance standards | ☐ | ☐ |
| Fulfil your slogan's promise | ☐ | ☐ |

# CHAPTER 9
# GO THE EXTRA MILE

In a place where so many service providers are trying to find every possible way to exert the least effort possible, you can stand out by simply doing a little more. Instead of just doing the minimum required, delight your customers by exceeding their expectations.

Of your own initiative, anticipate their needs before they ask, offer them something that they will actually enjoy but may not have thought to ask for. Do something that may be a little outside your job description but, that will greatly increase a customer's level of satisfaction.

Commit yourself to providing customer solutions. More times than not, what we hear coming from service providers is long lists of all the things they cannot do for us and why. Instead, make saying yes to customers a habit, part of your company's culture. Sometimes it might mean going just a little out of your way but the results will far outweigh the effort you put in. Customers who feel like you more than cater to their needs will tell their family and friends about you. So will the customers who think you are doing an awful job. This second group however, will make it a point to warn the people they know to stay away from you. Why not do your best to cause customers to say nothing but positive things about you and your business?

Word of mouth advertising is an effective and incredibly cost-efficient tool. The only way to obtain it however; is to give customers something worth talking about – why not make that something positive? Personal endorsements and recommendations will go much further in convincing a new customer to pay you a visit in person or online, simply because they are so much more credible than paid advertising. On a rainy day offer to walk that customer back to their car under your umbrella. Offer to help that parent with a child who looks like they are having a hard time juggling their groceries and the little toddler at the same time. Help roll that elderly traveller's rolling suitcase to the kerb where their ride is waiting. Offer a ride to the frazzled customer who is running late for an appointment but finds she has a flat tyre. Proactively look for opportunities to say, "Yes, it will be my pleasure," and look for opportunities to be helpful. Front line employees are busy looking for ways to do as little as possible with and for customers, and say "no" far too easily and far too often. "No, you cannot substitute boiled potatoes for mashed potatoes." "No, that is not my department." "No, I cannot tell you when you will be reconnected." We have all heard the responses that make us cringe and ask for a manager or supervisor, or wish there was an alternative provider.

Train your employees to think of ways to eliminate the word "no" from their vocabulary when dealing with customers and give employees the freedom to take quick decisions without having to check with a supervisor each time, provided the decisions will delight the customer. Remember that a happy customer is a freely spending customer and an effective advertisement that you do not have to pay for.

## Be flexible

Do your employees rigidly follow procedure even when circumstances justify modifications? My friend Joy was in a hurry to obtain a visa to a European country. She had just received an unexpected conference invitation and hoped to depart over the weekend. That Thursday morning, Joy submitted a complete visa application to the country's embassy in Kampala with an appeal for expedited processing. On Friday, Joy returned to the embassy for her passport. When she informed an embassy employee that she had dropped off her passport the day before, the employee had just seven words for her, "You can't get it in a day!" Case closed. Frustrated and with nowhere to turn, Joy called her host in Europe pleading for support. A call from Joy's European host to the embassy achieved nothing. The passport would be ready on Monday.

A disappointed Joy therefore rescheduled her Sunday flight and on Monday morning retrieved her passport from the country's embassy.

Upon inspecting her visa, Joy found that it actually had been issued on Friday. So why was she made to wait until Monday to pick it up? Simply because someone believed, "You can't get it in a day!" A little flexibility and a call on Friday would have made a big difference and saved Joy $250 in ticket change fees.

## Value orderliness

On a trip out of one of East Africa's international airports, I paid special attention to the plane boarding process, in a bid to understand why I always feel like I am either witnessing or participating in a mini-stampede whenever I board a plane there. As boarding time approached, the departing passengers in the gate area started gathering around the exit door leading to the plane, creating an impenetrable barrier.

At boarding time, an airport handling service employee invited all passengers travelling with children or requiring special assistance to begin boarding the plane. The invitation was issued in a large room without the use of a microphone. I highly doubt that any of the passengers in the invited categories actually heard the announcement; I did not see any of them heading towards the front of the human sea blocking the exit door. Or perhaps they realized that any attempts to get through the human sea would be futile and so simply did not bother.

In response to the priority boarding call, the human sea at the exit door simply pushed its way out with absolutely no consideration for priority boarding categories and the possibility of a pleasant and orderly boarding process.

This is the final customer service experience that airport offers departing airline passengers and it bears plenty of room for improvement. The simple use of a microphone and a request to passengers to line up in an orderly fashion would go a long way in making the boarding process a pleasant one. Put in a little extra effort to leave a positive lasting memory!

## Go beyond your job description

"That isn't my job!" How many times has someone said this to us or worse still, how many times have we said it ourselves? More often than not, what it really means is, "Get someone else to do that for you, not me!" I was shopping in one of our supermarkets and wanted to purchase a fan that was on a shelf too high for me to reach. I therefore went in search of a shop attendant to help get the fan down for me.

Two aisles away, I found a young man in the supermarket's employee uniform, stocking shelves. I asked him to come and help me, fully expecting him to immediately walk back to the fan aisle with me. Imagine my surprise when the young man walked away, telling me he was going to look for someone else to help me. "That isn't my job!" his words and actions seemed to say. I watched him walk almost the full length of the store before I turned around to look for another attendant. Fortunately, the next attendant I approached came to my assistance immediately, as previously expected.

Same store location, same day, but two completely different attitudes towards serving customers. How do your employees respond to customer requests for help? It should be every employee's responsibility to come to a customer's aid, even in an area where it is not the employee's job.

## Provide solutions

Do your employees seek to provide solutions? Zik who lives in Kuwait and two of his Kampala friends decided they had to attend the year's first Grand Prix Formula 1™ race in Bahrain. Since Zik lives in the region, he offered to book hotel rooms and purchase event tickets on his friends' behalf. The Kampala friends had to obtain their visas in advance and because Bahrain hotels offer incoming guests 48 hour visa processing, this would not be a problem. Visa applications were submitted a month in advance but three weeks later, the visas had not been issued. Zik therefore called the hotel every day that fourth week to follow up, to no avail. When Zik and his family arrived in Bahrain the Thursday before the race, his Kampala friends' visas had still not been issued. Now in Islamic nations, Friday is just like our Sunday. That being the case, without making any effort whatsoever, Kamal the hotel employee Zik had called all week, advised him to cancel his friends' hotel rooms and accept a refund.

Instead of following up with Bahrain immigration to find out why visas normally issued within 48 hours had not been issued for four weeks, Kamal simply made absolutely no effort to find a solution. Sounds like our part of the world! Just a simple phone call from the hotel to Immigration on behalf of incoming guests would have provided an answer.

## Plan customer care deliberately

I once had the pleasure of being treated like a valued customer in a shop I had never been to before. Given the stiff competition offered by online options, US brick and mortar bookshops like the then national chain Borders, take great pains to keep customers walking in. No sooner had I wandered into a US Borders, than a smiling associate greeted me, introduced herself and asked if she could help me find anything in particular.

To my vague answer about easy fish recipes, Jennifer escorted me to a bookshelf where she selected a specific book, turned to her favourite fish recipe and explained why she recommended it. "Let me know if I can help you find anything else," she said as she walked away. Jennifer seemed so keen to help and so knowledgeable that after scanning a few recipes, I bought the book she recommended. I later learned that associate lines are pre-scripted, customer interactions timed and associate product knowledge regularly tested.

Jennifer's deliberate attention to my needs resulted in a sale. Do you plan your customer care deliberately and evaluate employees on how well they perform against predetermined measures?

## Turn clients into raving fans

Last year, my friend Dolores finally got her house construction feet wet by finding an architect to design her dream house. It took the first architect Dolores worked with one meeting to turn down the assignment. Finding Dolores to be "too exacting", the first architect recommended

# KEEPING CUSTOMERS

*Go beyond your job description*

a boutique architectural firm, as a suitable replacement. Jesse, the Lead Architect so impressed Dolores at their first meeting that ever since, Dolores has inundated any friend who will listen with stories about how good her architect is. Truly unique house designs, three dimensional drawings, miniature house models for easy visualization, creative problem solving, openness to client ideas, punctuality and integrity are some of the attributes Dolores raves on and on about, as she subjects every unsuspecting friend who crosses her path to her architect's drawings of her dream house. Just before Christmas that year, Dolores called to let me know that the firm had invited her to a client appreciation Christmas dinner. Clearly, the firm's already high ranking with Dolores had just been raised another notch. We all ought to turn customers into raving fans who recommend us to everyone; and we should learn to demonstrate client appreciation in unexpected ways.

## Do the unexpected

Following a memorable album launch by one of Uganda's jazz musicians, my friends and I were unable to purchase the music on CD because the CDs were sold out. Wanting to alleviate our frustration, Tricia, who works for the musician, came to our rescue by putting us in touch with their sales department. My call to Ben Baker was met with an enthusiastic promise to deliver the CDs to my office. On the designated delivery day, Ben was running late.

But instead of leaving me in the dark as so many would have, he politely called to let me know where he was and when he would be at my office. Upon arrival, he informed me that they normally did not offer personal delivery but since I had asked, he had made it happen, for no charge.

It is amazing what a big impression a small unexpected gesture will make on a customer. Ben Baker demonstrated professionalism and went out of his way to delight me. Reward your employees for coming up with creative ways to impress customers in unexpected yet much appreciated ways.

## Go beyond sorry

Does your company go beyond sorry? Not wanting to wait in line in an international airline's always crowded Kampala office, I e-mailed Paul one of that airline's reservations agents, requesting a travel itinerary. Two days later, I had no response so my office contacted the airline, submitting my request to Lydia. This ticket booking process typically takes a few e-mails to and fro before an acceptable itinerary and price are finally identified. Lydia and I were engaged in just that, when the Icelandic cloud of volcanic ash shut down the European skies, halted over 100,000 scheduled flights and rendered the resulting stranded travellers a top priority for every affected airline. Consequently, I did not hear from Lydia for a few days.

When she eventually contacted me, Lydia's e-mail included an apology for her silence owing to prevailing circumstances, an acceptable itinerary and best of all, the suggestion that I purchase my ticket online and save $50. On the same day, I finally heard from Paul. He too apologized for not replying sooner. He had been away on leave, returning to the office just in time for the crisis. Like Lydia, he also suggested I book my ticket online for faster service and provided instructions. I followed their advice and ten minutes later had my e-ticket receipt in hand, having paid $50 less than I would have if the agents had completed the transaction.

I was delighted by the reservation agents' responses to me. They went beyond apologizing and offered me an efficient, cost-saving solution too. How does your company offer customers a little more than expected?

## Influence customers with simple actions

Sheila and I were at an early morning meeting in the residents' lounge of one of Kampala's hotels when a pastry chef walked in to fill the pastry display case with a variety of freshly baked cakes. With several items on our agenda that morning, Sheila and I were determined not to give in to any distractions. We therefore did our best to ignore the chef as she walked by, but first our noses then our eyes betrayed us. As she arranged the cakes in the display case, Beatrice the pastry chef looked over and said hello. No sooner had we responded than I heard myself asking Beatrice if anyone had conducted taste tests on the cakes that morning.

Amused by my thinly veiled request, Beatrice smiled and asked a nearby waitress to serve us each a slice of the cake of our choice. Sheila and I derived such immense enjoyment from our unexpected treat that we have inundated our families and friends with countless recommendations that they visit the hotel. Additionally, both Sheila and I are making increasingly more frequent purchases from the hotel's bakery. Beatrice's simple gesture delighted us, creating a ripple effect that can only benefit the hotel.

## Offer solutions

Are some of the people you hire costing you lost sales? My friend William, a devoted and loyal customer of one of our supermarkets, happened to be walking past his favourite supermarket when he decided it would be a good place for him to purchase airtime. At the supermarket entrance, the plain clothes security officer responsible for scanning everyone as they entered, stopped William to let him know that he could not enter the supermarket with his computer bag.

When William innocently asked where he could leave it, the security officer informed William that he simply would not be allowed to get past that particular point, and that was the end of the story. Interestingly enough, a uniformed guard who happened to overhear the exchange came to William's rescue. The uniformed guard showed William where he could leave his bag before entering the supermarket and as they headed to that location, William let slip that as a loyal customer, he was completely disappointed by the rude treatment he had received especially since all he wanted was airtime. The helpful uniformed guard then showed William a jewellery shop where he could purchase airtime, without having to leave his bag behind. I shudder to think of the number of customers that have suffered a negative experience at the hands of that supermarket's unhelpful security officer, and the resulting value of lost sales.

Instead of ignoring William's question and having the audacity to rudely turn him away empty-handed, the security officer ought to have listened to William's request and offered him a solution instead of a flat "no!" It took a passer-by to offer a helpful solution. Who monitors your staff to ensure that they are not costing you business by refusing to be helpful?

## Observe customers attentively

A seemingly small gesture could make a big difference for a customer. Alice has shopped at a small neighbourhood fresh produce stall for several years. On a typical shopping day, Alice parks her car a few feet away, walks briskly to the stall, selects and purchases fresh produce then walks back to her car. When Alice was expecting a child, she gained not a little weight, which slowed down her walk. Noticing this, one of the stall attendants suggested that Alice start dropping off her shopping list the day before she needed the produce.

The following day, all Alice would have to do was drive up to the stall, an attendant would then bring the pre-selected produce to the vehicle and collect payment. This worked smoothly for several weeks until one Friday, when Alice was too indisposed to drop off her list. To Alice's appreciative delight however, when her husband later stopped at the stall to purchase what he thought they needed, the attendant put together a basket of "the usual," which turned out to be everything Alice would have listed.

Attentive observation equipped the staff at that stall to provide unsolicited yet well appreciated customer solutions. How might you offer unsolicited yet welcome and relevant gestures to help make customers enjoy their experience with you more?

## Spot opportunities to help

After our lunch at one of Kampala's cafes, my friend Stella and I walked to our parked vehicles only to discover that Stella's car had a flat tyre. Now just that morning, Stella had taken her car's boot key off her key chain. She therefore could not retrieve her spare tire. Since I had to rush back to work, I offered to drive Stella and her flat tyre one-way to the nearest petrol station.

As we weighed the various means by which Stella and the repaired tyre could get back to the cafe, Mr. Mukasa, a cafe driver stopped by and asked us what was going on. Stella explained the situation, finishing with the dilemma at hand. Mr. Mukasa immediately instructed one of the other cafe drivers to drive Stella and the tyre to the nearest petrol station, wait while the tyre was repaired and bring Stella and the tyre back. Smiling at our surprised expressions, Mr. Mukasa remarked "You are our customers! Without you, where would we be?" Less than 45 minutes later, Stella was driving home.

Mr. Mukasa's thoughtfulness in extending service well beyond the lunch we had paid for, moved Stella deeply enough to guarantee the cafe her devoted loyalty. Spot opportunities to be helpful to your customers. Sometimes, these opportunities may lie just outside the scope of your business definition, but still be within easy reach.

## Fulfil reasonable customer requests

I was supposed to attend two three-day workshops at the same time, hosted at two different hotels across the road from each other. One of hotel A's gates that faces hotel B however, is always locked. Within the locked gate, the large gate is reserved for VIPs and the small pedestrian gate beside it is simply never opened. Customers have to use an alternative entrance that is quite a distance away. This makes for rather long walks between the two hotels for non-VIPs like me. On workshop day two, having walked for what felt like at least four kilometres as I crisscrossed between the two hotels the day before, I had had enough. So I asked a smiling receptionist at the hotel with the locked VIP gate if there was even a remote chance that the small gate right by the VIP gate could be unlocked for me, to save me the long walk back to the hotel on the other side of the street.

To my surprise and utter delight, Jackson the duty manager came to unlock the small gate and informed me that it was his absolute pleasure to do so. Since my office happens to be in the same vicinity, Jackson even gave me his cell phone number so that I could call him should I ever need to use the small gate again. That hotel definitely takes customer service very seriously, to the point where even managers find no customer request too small or too menial. Does your business fit into the same category?

## Remember customer details

After a two year stint out of the country, my friend Olive and her children walked into their neighbourhood butchery. Sara the shop attendant welcomed them with a huge smile and almost jumped for joy as she excitedly called out the girls' names and hurried around the counter to extend even warmer greetings. When Olive asked for bread, Sara rushed to the bread section and without prompting selected a loaf of Olive's favourite bread, even remembering to slice it.

A few days later, Olive drove back to the butchery and asked one of her daughters to run in for sausages. Seconds later, Olive's daughter was back with an apologetic Sara. Unfortunately, the family's favourite sausages were out of stock but would Olive mind sampling this other type that Sara had brought to the car and that she highly recommended?

Sara made these customers feel special by remembering their names and preferences even after two long years. Sara treats customers like family and cheerfully offers helpful solutions. In Olive's own words, "Sara never walks, she sort of springs as she efficiently serves her customers, all day, every day." Although there are several places Olive could go for good whole wheat bread, clean fish and a variety of cuts of meat, she prefers to go to Sara. Do any of your customers feel that way about you?

## Proactively find solutions

A couple of the tenants in our office building run businesses that involve a large number of vehicles. At times, the vehicles crowd our small parking lot, leaving some tenants with nowhere to park. The situation is aggravated every time individuals attending a function at one of the nearby hotels decide to park in our compound. My numerous complaints to both our landlord and our then security guard proved fruitless, so I resigned myself to giving the security guard a little talk each time I could not find a place to park my car.

Fortunately, after a few months of this, we got a new security guard – Augustino. Unlike his predecessor, Augustino asked everyone who drove into our compound where they were going. Augustino would only let tenants or people who had meetings with tenants enter the compound and park. More importantly for me, on his own initiative Augustino made a portable wooden sign post on which he painted my license plate number. He uses the sign to reserve parking for me and has effectively terminated my parking complaints.

Augustino proactively solved our parking situation and found me a customized solution. Do you give your employees enough leeway to come up with creative solutions to please customers?

## Offer creative solutions

How do you go out of your way to keep customers satisfied? When my brother and his family left for an overseas trip, they hired a taxi driver they had never used before for the ride to the airport. The courteous driver was punctual and when he dropped them off at the airport, asked them not to pay him until they returned, an excellent way of ensuring that my brother's family called him for the ride home from the airport. On returning, my brother's family had far too much luggage to fit in the same taxi that had been used for the ride to the airport. Upon realizing that another vehicle was required, the resourceful taxi driver phoned a friend who immediately drove to the airport and loaded the luggage into his car. The whole exercise was completed in less than 20 minutes and at no extra cost to my brother.

The driver's resourcefulness as well as his decision not to charge for the extra vehicle definitely guarantee him my brother and his family's unwavering loyalty on all their frequent trips to and from the airport.

# KEEPING CUSTOMERS

*Spot opportunities to help*

## Points to Ponder

1. What unexpected and creative solution have you recently provided to a customer? What was the customer's response?

2. How much liberty do members of your team have to go outside their job description in order to positively enhance an interaction with a customer?

3. What will it take for you to give team members the liberty to go outside their job description to delight a customer?

4. How will you encourage team members to go past the expected, in their delivery of services to customers?

5. What recognition do you provide to team members who customers constantly compliment or give you positive feedback about?

6. When was the most recent time you said "No" to a customer? How could you have turned that no into a yes?

## To Do List

- At your next staff meeting ask members of your team to share examples of how they went an extra mile for a customer in the last month. If no one has a story to share, that is a clear indication that your organization makes no extra effort at all, to please its customers. If this is the case, make going an extra mile one of your objectives for the month ahead. If however, there are plenty of stories to share, that is a good sign. Publicly commend the employees for their achievement.

- Make a long term commitment to reward yourself and your team for saying "Yes!" to a customer. What kind of rewards will you offer?

## How Are You Doing?

If a principle is one that you currently practice, put a tick (√) in the Yes column. If a principle is one you need to work on, put a tick in the No column.

| Go the Extra Mile | Yes | No |
|---|---|---|
| Be flexible | | |
| Value orderliness | | |
| Go beyond your job description | | |
| Plan customer care deliberately | | |
| Turn clients into raving fans | | |
| Do the unexpected | | |
| Go beyond sorry | | |
| Influence customers with simple actions | | |
| Offer creative solutions | | |
| Observe customers attentively | | |
| Spot opportunities to help | | |
| Fulfil reasonable customer requests | | |
| Remember customer details | | |
| Proactively find solutions | | |

# CHAPTER 10
# VALUE FEEDBACK

Communication is a two-way street involving both giving and receiving. If we are to create, build and maintain strong relationships with our customers, the demonstration of the ability not just to speak, but more importantly to listen and really hear what our customers are saying is imperative. Many service providers in our part of the world however simply do not bother to offer customers an opportunity to speak to them. When frustrated customers seize the opportunity on their own and provide feedback which if listened to might actually contribute to growing a company's customer base and sales, the customers' comments are commonly brushed aside. Service providers will do well to listen and take action accordingly.

Always thank the customer, irrespective of whether you agree with them or not. Never go on the defensive. Weigh the information provided – it might not always be well intended - and find a means of responding politely and appropriately. Offer the customer a solution or find a way to get the company to respond. If one customer has a problem with something you do, it is not likely that they are the only one. Instead of letting customers slip away from you because the vast majority of them would rather simply walk away than tell you what they do not appreciate, take heed of what the few who do come forward tell you. In an increasingly more competitive market place, customers who let you know how you are doing will help you stay ahead of the competition, provided you act in a timely fashion on the information they share with you.

View feedback as an opportunity, not a threat and actively seek to obtain and act on it. A wide variety of tools for collecting all kinds of feedback exist for example, customer service desks or telephone help lines, suggestion boxes, written surveys, focus groups and even mystery shoppers. Additionally, in today's electronic age, customer feedback may also be easily obtained through text messages, e-mail or even on social networking pages. From the many available, accessible and affordable tools, choose the means that will be the most effective for both your customers and your business. Do not confine yourself to using a tool however, as even just asking a customer a simple conversational question like what they would like to see your company do differently, will result in a wealth of useful and valuable information.

In order to get the most meaningful feedback, rather than asking close-ended questions that a customer can respond to with either "yes" or "no," ask open-ended questions that begin with words like how, what, where, why, when, and who; the standard investigative questions. By asking open-ended questions, you give your respondent plenty of room to explain their position and you therefore learn a lot more. To illustrate, instead of asking "Do you like this menu?" to which the answer is yes or no, ask "What do you like about this menu?" The respondent will have to explain what they like about the menu, giving you useful insights on what to keep on the menu and what to discard. Similarly, instead of asking: "Will you return to this supermarket?" Ask the same question in a manner that will draw an explanation from your customer – "Why will you return to this supermarket?" The respondent will have no choice but to provide you with some valuable information about why they will be back.

If you either seek or receive customer feedback, make sure you honour it by acting on it. Let acting on customer feedback become your secret means of advancement and business growth.

## Spend time with customers

During our second week at a leading hotel in Lusaka, Musole, the Front Office Manager spotted a group of us in the hotel lounge and decided that we presented an excellent opportunity for her to easily obtain immediate, rich and detailed customer feedback. Musole therefore approached us and asked if we were enjoying our stay. Seven eager respondents bombarded her with their answers, causing Musole to excuse herself so she could obtain a notebook to document all our responses. She then spent the next 30 minutes with us, recording what was working well, what had gone wrong and even brainstorming potential solutions. Where possible, Musole provided immediate solutions, for example a 50 percent discount on our daily internet rate. Where unable to provide immediate solutions, Musole assured us things would change before we checked out of the hotel. Indeed, the guests who complained about used items in their rooms not being consistently replaced with fresh ones for example, sugar and coffee sachets and a variety of bathroom items, reported a positive change. In response to Musole's quick thinking, each interviewed guest is now highly likely to suggest that hotel to friends seeking Lusaka hotel recommendations.

Musole recognized an opportunity to gain valuable customer feedback and provide immediate solutions where possible. The time we spent with her and the results effectively overshadowed any preceding negative experiences.

## Find easy ways to obtain feedback

Do your customers find it easy to give you feedback? It was my second week at another leading hotel in Lusaka, Zambia where I was attending a workshop for 35 trade experts from eight African countries. At the end of our first week, several of us had had both negative and positive experiences that would have been interesting for hotel management to hear about. There was however, no visible means for us to provide feedback. With no easy way to register our complaints and compliments, we would be leaving the hotel without sharing this valuable information with the right audience. Guests do receive a feedback form the day before they check out of the hotel but, the space allocated for feedback is far too small to accommodate the detailed comments that some guests are willing to offer and that the hotel would find informative. Given the related degrees of difficulty, many of us would probably have ended up ignoring the feedback form, preferring to tell family and friends about all our negative hotel experiences while conveniently ignoring the positive ones.

Businesses everywhere miss out on obtaining valuable customer feedback by not providing a user-friendly means of collecting it. Find creative ways to make it easy for customers to tell you how things are going. Stop them and ask them if there is anything you can do to make their experience more comfortable or enjoyable. Provide simple feedback forms that are easy to fill out and leave them in a visible location, send a follow-up e-mail asking what you might do to make the next visit more enjoyable. Many customers will be happy to provide the information and they will be even happier when they return and find you actually implemented their suggestions. That can only be good for business!

## Track customer feedback

During difficult financial times, one would expect a company to do everything within its power to stretch its valuable resources. Interestingly enough, this is not always the case. Just as my company's subscription to a regional weekly newspaper was about to expire, our office received two calls from the paper. Each call reminded us to renew our subscription and each caller was informed that we had opted to cancel our subscription. To be doubly sure, we also did not complete the paper's subscription renewal form. A full year later, in spite of the numerous calls we made to the newspaper's offices reminding them that we were no longer subscribers, as well as assurances from the newspaper's staff that delivery would stop, weekly delivery continued.

If this happened to us, my guess is that it happened to other people too. Errors like this add up and in the long run, will prove costly to the newspaper. Why continue the unsolicited, dedicated weekly delivery of a newspaper when a customer has opted not to renew their subscription?

## Apply customer feedback

As a once faithful subscriber to a weekly regional newspaper, I used to look forward to reading my paper every Monday morning. In my opinion, the paper provided an excellent overview of regional business news.

I therefore chose to buy the paper because I valued the information it held. Secondly, I chose to subscribe to the paper because delivery was guaranteed and finally, I subscribed because I always want to be the first person to read my own newspaper.

To start with, my Monday morning paper was always pushed under my office door and stapled closed with a typed label bearing my name and address. For several weeks at one point however, the manner of delivery changed. The paper was delivered to our building's lobby, without a staple and with my name scribbled in ink across the top. On two separate occasions since the change, my enjoyable Monday morning reading experience was marred by the unsightly underlining of various articles by someone in the lobby who always read my newspaper before me. Subsequently, I made at least four phone calls to request that the paper be stapled before delivery. Each time, a promise to staple was made but never implemented.

The paper is to blame for a decline in service that compromised a customer's enjoyable reading experience and for not following through on promises made to correct their mistake. The paper should have documented our request, addressed it and made an effort to find out if our concerns had been addressed.

## Accommodate reasonable customer requests

Have you ever had to badger someone you were paying for a service into doing what you were paying them for? Having failed to arrest the attention of sign-makers in the city, I resorted to working with Festo, an upcountry freelance sign-writer instead. Recommended by a colleague, Festo seemed to understand that all he had to do was duplicate the artwork provided, but on a much larger scale. The company logo was to be the primary focus and the first row of text had to be twice the size of the text on the second row. Festo had 48 hours to create stencils for my approval.

In spite of having a reference sheet to look at, Festo created stencils depicting text that was all the same size. When I calmly attempted to explain the changes I wanted, instead of listening, Festo spoke over me, loudly and repeatedly, informing me that all the letters had to be the same size to fill up the board. Was I dreaming or was the sign-writer trying to redesign my sign? Just to get Festo to stop talking, I was forced to stand up and pound the table with my fist. The colleague who had recommended him had to pull Festo aside and warn him that unless he cooperated, he would be losing a customer.

Festo tried to forcefully impose his personal tastes and preferences on me, almost causing me to abandon the transaction. A better course of action would have been to follow the instructions I provided (to the letter) and listen to my point of view as opposed to shouting and trying to force his views about my sign down my throat!

## Seek and utilize customer feedback

Agility to respond – now there's a quality every company should strive to have! Naturally it is much easier for a small company (with the right resources) to quickly respond to customer feedback than it is for a large one. There are fewer people to get permission and approval from.

Selly recently launched a pie-making and delivery business. Her entire first week of operation was devoted purely to getting customer feedback. Selly had planned to begin by selling her meat pies at US$0.25 each. In response to customer feedback however, she decided to launch both meat and vegetable pies at the lower price of US$0.20. She is now making money off a devoted and satisfied customer base.

Everyone in business should actively seek and act on customer feedback. After all, we are in business to make as big a profit as possible by meeting our customers' needs. Stay in touch with your customers' dynamic needs by keeping the lines of communication open.

## Take corrective measures quickly

When customers offer negative feedback, if found to be true, does your company take corrective measures and if yes, how quickly? On two occasions, each within weeks of each other, Maggie found herself filling out a restaurant feedback form on a fast food company's website. Maggie felt it was her responsibility to notify corporate headquarters about the hamburgers being sold in her neighbourhood. Both times, the complaint was the same – when she lifted the top section of the bun off her hamburger, the exposed meat patty looked like someone had taken a bite out of it. My comment to Maggie was that the person who assembled the hamburgers was probably just a little careless and accidentally tore the patties while placing them on the buns. Maggie's position however, was that there should have been absolutely nothing about the hamburgers to discourage her from eating them. She was further disappointed to find that several weeks after filing her first complaint, when she ordered the same hamburger at the same restaurant, nothing had changed.

The restaurant should have viewed the feedback as important and taken corrective measures as soon as possible. Providing a section on their website where customers can file complaints gives the false impression that they actually care about hearing customer feedback. If no action seems to be taken when feedback is provided, customers will soon stop providing it. Act on customer feedback immediately and avoid having disappointed customers discourage friends and family from doing business with you.

## Act on customer feedback

Jackie decided to go on yet another mystery diet. All she revealed about it was that it focused on healthy, organic foods, with eggs featuring dominantly. Jackie therefore soon became something of a self-made expert on the local egg brands sold in Kampala's supermarkets. "Nature's Foods" stood out for Jackie almost immediately because the label states "Our egg is healthier & has more nutrients due to FULL organic practice, hygiene management & local herbs used for disease prevention & control." While Jackie greatly appreciated the eggs' flavour, the hygiene management claim was questionable. Each individual egg invariably boasted some degree of organic waste matter on its shell.

After months of this, Jackie finally got tired of washing the eggs each time she purchased them. She therefore called the phone number on the egg tray and suggested to a very accommodating proprietor that the eggs be cleaned prior to packing. Jackie's suggestion was warmly received and subsequently implemented. Jackie happily reports that she no longer has to wash Nature's Foods eggs after purchase.

Nature's Foods acted on a stranger's feedback and ended up presenting a much more attractive product. This can only work in the company's favour, contributing to a positive brand image.

## Receive and respond to feedback

My friends and I were visiting a restaurant that we had not been to in a long time, clinging to old memories of good service. I ordered my all-time favourite, "Sausages and Mash". The disappointment began when my mashed potatoes were served on a small side plate with neither the onions nor the gravy listed on the menu. My request for gravy was met with the information that I had to pay for it. After I challenged the waiter, he brought me what must be the restaurant's smallest serving bowl, holding about six tablespoons of gravy. In the past, enough gravy to drown the entire serving of mashed potatoes was served in a gravy boat.

Like Oliver Twist, I had to ask for more. Instead of accommodating a paying customer's simple request, the supervisor on duty proceeded to talk over me, explaining how expensive it was to make the gravy because "it includes wine and should be used like chutney." I could therefore pay US$1.00 for more. Needless to say, I rejected his offer because I believe every dish on a restaurant's menu should be served correctly, with everything in the right proportions.

The restaurant compromised meal quality in a bid to make a few extra shillings and clearly the manner in which the employees handled customer requests had deteriorated atrociously over the months. I have not been back to that particular restaurant since then, nor do I plan to. Aim to retain not chase customers away.

## Implement feedback and cultivate customer loyalty

Do you ever think about the simple actions that cultivate customer loyalty? Liz visited one of Kampala's new cafes in a popular mall. A smiling James took her order and quickly returned with lukewarm coffee served in a cup. Looking around, Liz noticed a few tables with teapots so she called James back and asked him to heat her coffee and serve it in a teapot. Not knowing what to do, the helpful James immediately summoned a manager. The manager informed Liz that only tea was served in teapots. Coffee was always served in cups. When Liz insisted that she would pay more if she had to in order to get her coffee heated and served in a teapot, the manager obligingly agreed, at no extra charge.

# KEEPING CUSTOMERS

*Appreciate feedback*

The staff listened to a customer's simple request and readily fulfilled it. Liz will definitely remain a loyal customer and is already recommending that cafe to all her friends.

## Respond to and encourage more feedback

One April, searching for back-to-school bargains, Helen's daughters headed to Kikuubo, a very large and incredibly busy Kampala open air market. The young ladies were thrilled to purchase three reams of Rotatrim photocopying paper at just US$4.00 each, instead of the price in other parts of town; US$ 6.00. It turned out however that one of the three perfectly sealed reams held only 30 sheets of white photocopying paper and hundreds of sheets of coloured duplicating paper. Helen therefore escorted her girls back to Kikuubo, looking for the trader her daughters had bought the paper from.

It was however, impossible to locate the offender in the overwhelming human sea that floods Kikuubo. Knowing full well that they do not issue receipts; the traders in that section of the market jeeringly challenged Helen to produce one.

Helen dutifully reported the incident to our national bureau of standards. She filled out a Consumer Complaint Reception form and received assurances that the responsible officers would survey the identified location. During the next six months, Helen called the bureau three times, to learn what had transpired. Each time, an employee recorded Helen's contact information, promising that an officer would be in touch but no call ever came.

A lack of responsiveness only serves to discourage dutiful citizens from reporting purchases of counterfeit products. Agencies responsible for overseeing product quality ought to offer the public a quality service too.

## View feedback as an opportunity

How does your company respond to feedback? Some companies go on the defensive and challenge the authenticity of the feedback they receive. Others use the feedback as a means of aligning employee behaviour

# KEEPING CUSTOMERS

*Act on feedback*

with the desired company image. When Management received information of their petrol station mechanic's unsuccessful attempts to cheat a customer by charging more than a vehicle servicing was worth, that company's Sales Department responded immediately. The company apologized for the mechanic's completely unacceptable behaviour and asked the customer to identify the individual responsible so disciplinary action could be taken.

The mechanic was asked to write an apology letter to the customer and make a cash contribution to the customer's favourite charity in the amount he had sought to obtain. The company also instructed its entire petrol station network to look out for employees involved in similar practices and provided the victimized customer a number to call whenever she had any additional feedback for the company.

Constantly embracing and acting on feedback will put you in a strong position with your customers. View feedback as an opportunity to both connect with and serve customers better.

## Reward customers for feedback

Do you reward, punish or ignore customers who offer your company feedback? In response to two e-mailed complaints to a US fast food company over hamburgers he had purchased at his neighbourhood restaurant, Gerald a US-based friend immediately received coupons for free replacement meals. Subsequently, Gerald began receiving coupons for complimentary samples whenever the company advertised a new product that year. Gerald actually ended up using all the complimentary coupons and each time he was in the restaurant, even ordered a few other additional items that he otherwise might not have thought of trying.

The complimentary coupons convinced Gerald that his feedback was well appreciated and also made him feel like an insider who gets to sample new products as soon as they are launched. How do you handle customers who provide you with feedback?

## Accept rejection gracefully

How do you handle rejection from potential customers? A group of my friends and I were at the Source of the Nile for a meeting. As soon as we sat down at a table in one of the restaurants, a young man called Ken approached us, offering three different boat ride options. Although Ken's prices seemed high, we patiently listened to him and then politely asked him to reconsider his rates while we had our meeting. After our meeting we would be interested in hearing his revised rates. During the three hour meeting, one of us secured a boat ride from one of Ken's competitors at US$15 less than Ken's best offer. When our meeting ended, Ken informed us that his prices were fixed. We thanked him, let him know we had an alternative and walked towards his competitor. Ken followed us, insisting with ever increasing aggression that his was the only ride available. He then began shouting in what seemed like three different local languages; berating our boat operator for "stealing" his customers and ordering him to "return" us. Fortunately, our boat operator stood his ground. We found out while we were on our boat ride, that Ken was simply a broker trying to make some money for doing no work at all.

When you offer an unattractive and therefore losing proposition, instead of attempting to use intimidation to get unimpressed customers back, find out what the customers did not like about your offer. Once you know why potential customers walked away, make the necessary changes so you do not miss out again. In this case, Ken should have made his price more reasonable.

## Points to Ponder

1. When was the last time you pro-actively solicited customer feedback?

2. What did you do with the feedback? Was collecting it merely a required exercise or did you put the information you gained to good use by making internal changes?

3. How do you respond when a customer motivated either by pain or pleasure voluntarily offers you negative or positive feedback?

4. What channels has your company made available for customer feedback? Are the channels visible to customers and easy to use?

5. What is your company's established position on customer feedback? Is it considered to be of value? If so, what does your company do with it?

6. Does your company proactively solicit customer feedback or do you wait for customer complaints that go unattended?

## To Do List

- In the week ahead, make it a point to ask every customer you interact with if they are happy doing business with you. Document their responses for a record of how you are doing. Make this a regular practice.

- Contact your most frequent customers and find out if there is something they would like you to do differently.

## How Are You Doing?

If a principle is one that you currently practice, put a tick (√) in the Yes column. If a principle is one you need to work on, put a tick in the No column.

| Value Feedback | Yes | No |
|---|---|---|
| Spend time with customers | | |
| Find easy ways to obtain feedback | | |
| Apply customer feedback | | |
| Accommodate reasonable requests | | |
| Seek and utilize customer feedback | | |
| Take corrective measures quickly | | |
| Act on customer feedback | | |
| Receive and respond to feedback | | |
| Implement feedback and cultivate loyalty | | |
| Respond to and encourage more feedback | | |
| View feedback as an opportunity | | |
| Reward customers for feedback | | |
| Accept rejection gracefully | | |

# CHAPTER 11
## COMPENSATE FOR ERRORS

Nobody wants to feel like they have been taken advantage of, least of all, a customer who pays good, hard-earned money for the goods and services they purchase. The positive feelings generated in a customer through compensation for a purchase that does not quite meet their expectations will in many cases, overcome the negative feelings generated by the earlier unpleasant experience. A compensated customer will not hesitate to recommend the provider who acknowledged that a mistake was made and turned it around. Neglecting to compensate unsatisfied customers in one way or another on the other hand, is a sure way of running your own negative publicity campaign.

Everyone knows that mistakes happen. Before you use that as an excuse however, have you done all you can to ensure that you consistently deliver a product or service that conforms to customer expectations? Do you have in-house quality standards and a means of measuring how well you are doing? This does not mean you have to invest in an expensive quality assessment and control system.

Ideally, you should ask your customers what they expect from you because it really is the customer who defines the quality they are looking for, not you. Once you have done this, invite members of your team to design a means of ensuring that defined quality standards are met. Naturally, for some of the more complex and regulated products and services, the national standards body should be invited to participate in the exercise. For other less complex businesses however, say for instance a hair salon, how will you ensure that the process to deliver a customer's desired hair colour is consistently the same and that the customer will never have to come back to ask you to re-do the job? How will you ensure that every bank teller's first words to each customer are words of greeting? Document the quality standards in every area and how they will be met. Train your employees on how to meet the quality standards; routinely monitor their performance and keep on re-training them until they get it right.

When the quality standards are breached and a mistake is made, quickly apologize and fix it. Instead of spending time and money trying to think of ways to avoid shouldering responsibility when a customer's expectations are not met, own the mistake and find a way to erase the negative experience from the customer's mind. When I was a child, one of the popular sayings on our school playground was "Sorry can't make a dead man live." I am not sure where it came from but it was the standard response whenever someone apologized for something they had done. The implication – you should not have done what you did in the first place. Short of actually replacing the toy you broke, your apology was essentially useless. We must have been onto something, even though we did not realize it.

For customers, the problem resolution process must be as simple as possible. Land's End, a Wisconsin, USA based clothing retailer is so confident of the quality of its products that all its guarantee policy says is "Guaranteed. Period." In other words, the minute you are unhappy with anything that you purchased from them, you are free to return it for a refund or exchange. There is no time limit after purchase e.g. returns and/or exchanges must be made within 45 days of purchase. What could be easier than that? In our part of the world however, if you look carefully at your receipts, you will find the following words at the bottom, in very small print: "Goods once sold, may not be returned." The companies that issue those receipts are really telling you to be their customer at your own risk!

With regards to compensation, restaurants typically offer you the disappointing meal you had on the house or invite you back for a complimentary meal, in the hopes that you will give them another opportunity to redeem themselves. When a flying insect hosted at your favourite cafe drowns in your coffee or fruit juice, any reputable establishment will replace your now unappealing drink at no cost to you. When the cleaning service you hired does not get to all the nooks and crannies you had hoped they would, they really ought to return at their own expense to do the job the way you expected them to.

An unhappy customer may be turned into a very happy customer by an apologetic service provider's demeanour and compensation in some form, be it an offer for a complimentary service in the future, the replacement of the offending product, or a discount. How difficult do you make it for customers to receive compensation?

> **Why you should address customer complaints[vii]**
>
> - The average unhappy customer will tell 8 to 16 people about it.
> - 91 percent of unhappy customers will never purchase a service from you again.
> - It costs 5 times more to attract a new customer than to keep a current one.
> - 82 to 95 percent of customers with a complaint will stay if you offer a remedy.

## Apologise for mistakes

While at a hotel in Maputo, Mozambique, a friend and I ordered a plate of beer battered fish and chips, among other things. I noted that our waiter did not write anything down and prepared myself to be duly impressed by his memorizing abilities. When he eventually reappeared with our meals, our waiter had creatively substituted the beer battered fish with a sword fish fillet. Although the sword fish fillet looked excellent, it certainly was not what had been ordered. My friend brought this to the attention of our waiter, who summoned his supervisor. The profusely apologetic supervisor immediately offered to replace the plate with the correct order and informed us that my friend's dinner would be on the house.

# COMPENSATE FOR ERRORS

*Correct mistakes*

The apology for the mistake, the immediate offer to replace the wrong order with the right one and the complimentary meal all rendered that Maputo hotel a winner in my book.

## Demonstrate your apology

Very few service providers in Uganda can be said to consistently provide commendably good service. I have however been impressed by the consistently good service the data network company that supports our office provides. While the company is a winner for many reasons, one of the reasons that stands out for me, is that irrespective of the employee I am dealing with – from the messenger all the way up to the CEO, I always receive the same brand of service - polite, immediate and effective. In the single incident over the years where my interaction with that company fell short of my expectations, the company acted swiftly to restore my confidence.

The customer service representative who handled a call I once made, dealt with me in a manner that I did not appreciate. My subsequent complaint to a senior manager resulted in a visit to my office by the representative in question. She came to personally apologize for her unsatisfactory service.

The unexpected visit erased my negative experience and convinced me of the company's commitment to providing good service. How does your company demonstrate remorse?

## Admit and correct mistakes

We decided on a supplier for our office door signs because of the professional manner in which they handled our inquiry and for their reasonable prices. The entire process from selecting the type of sign and colours we wanted, to reviewing the artwork before the signs were actually printed went quite smoothly. Within a week, our signs were ready for collection. Upon review however, we noticed that the ink had not been uniformly applied to the etching of our company's logo on the sign.

Some of the ink looked "streaky" for lack of a better description. Mala handled the situation professionally. In sharp contrast to the norm, she offered no defensive remarks. She simply agreed with my observations, apologized and promised to have the job re-done to our satisfaction.

Sure enough, several days later, a pleasant and cheerful employee delivered the new signs to our office.

Polite and prompt willingness to correct work that did not meet customer expectations was a rare treat indeed! How often do you respond positively to an unsatisfied customer? Your response will either keep your customers returning or chase them away.

## Rectify mistakes

More often than not, the person at whose hands you suffer unsatisfactory service is not the person to rectify the situation. You have to go "higher up" to seek redress. Following a disappointing and flippant conversation with the breeder of some poor quality goats a community group I work with had recently purchased, I contacted the non-government association that oversees the breeders' association. I reported what had transpired to Shamilah, the veterinary doctor in charge, and asked her to help get the community group's breeding centre back on the right track. Shamilah acknowledged the breeder's violation of association guidelines, called him to task for his actions and promised to rectify the situation. Shamilah then travelled to the breeding centre, physically inspected the goats, ascertained their poor condition as well as the absence of tags and records and finally, offered the community group a full refund in spite of incredibly strong opposition from the earlier mentioned breeder, who also happened to be the breeders' association chairman.

Shamilah acknowledged that the breeders' chairman had indeed violated sale guidelines, rectified the situation and effectively reversed actions that would have set the community group's breeding centre on a disastrous path. Does your company take full responsibility for mistakes made?

## Offer helpful responses

Is your company's help desk actually helpful? Norman a savvy social networker, once loaded US$ 2.50 worth of airtime on his mobile phone, just like he always did every three to four days. 30 minutes later Norman found he had a balance of less than US$0.01! Confused, Norman called his phone company's customer care number only to learn that Angela could not help him because the system was down. Angela promised to call Norman back in an hour but having heard that line several times before, Norman informed Angela that he did not believe her. Sure enough, Angela's call never came. So Norman loaded another US$2.50 and within a few minutes, through no effort of his own, Norman's airtime was down to US$1.25. Again, Norman called the phone company. The person he spoke to assured Norman that Norman's phone was faulty and that he needed to log out of Twitter and Facebook whenever he was not using them. Perturbed because he has always kept his social networking pages open at no extra charge, Norman stated as much. The response -"Maybe things have changed!" An exasperated Norman then emailed an inquiry to the e-mail address that the company lists on its website. No answer ever came. Fortunately however, Norman's "faulty" phone repaired itself and like before, he can now keep his social networking pages open for no additional charge.

Unhelpful customer care representatives, no e-mail response, no explanation, no apology and no refund – that is no way to conduct business. Ensure that your customer representatives know enough about your products to give meaningful responses. And if a customer seeks an explanation for unexplained charges, provide an answer and compensate them if the mistake indeed turns out to be the company's fault. Finally, at the very least, if you cannot respond to e-mails, do not advertise your e-mail address. The company should have e-mailed an immediate acknowledgement of receipt to Norman, followed by an answer to his query.

## Correct errors promptly

How promptly do you correct errors? For the two years since we were allocated our current water meter, we have paid our office water bills promptly. We were therefore rudely surprised when early one January morning a meter reader delivered a disconnection notice, claiming our account was in arrears. Fortunately, the person who handles all our bills happened to be in the office at the time, so he showed her two years' worth of water payment receipts. Declaring that we had been paying the wrong water bill for two years, the meter reader did not disconnect us and promised to report the confusion to Head Office. The next day however, our taps were dry so, one of our officers went to our water supplier's office and had a lengthy discussion with a customer care manager who appeared to understand that two different accounts had been mixed up. She promised to correct the error. Instead of a solution however, that month we received a US$ 250 bill, against an unknown meter number. In response to our written complaint, our water supplier sent a current statement of account showing all our payments for the past year until then, an account credit balance following our most recent payment and three new entries for the next month against an unknown meter number, amounting to US$250 which our supplier wanted us to pay right away.

Our provider simply was not willing to listen to our side of the story and yet, the whole situation arose out of sheer negligence on their part, in allocating us the wrong meter number. The problem was eventually resolved but we had to spend far too many of our valuable man-hours pursuing a solution and we certainly did not appreciate the provider's attitude. Had we had a choice, we would have switched providers. Enterprises should always offer their customers a listening ear, a helping hand and even some form of apologetic compensation for inconveniences like this, more especially if the error can be traced back to the provider.

## Repair or replace faulty products

Isaac, a first year engineering student at Makerere University Kampala excitedly purchased an Acer laptop from an electronics retailer in Kampala for US$325. It was rather late on a Saturday evening so the shop attendant quickly switched the laptop on and off and informed Isaac that the price included a one year guarantee. That night, an eager

Isaac switched on his new laptop, only to encounter a blinking screen. Believing he had a guarantee, Isaac took the laptop back to the retailer the following Monday, where Saturday's attendant told him the laptop would be replaced in two weeks. Two weeks later, Isaac returned to the shop and was asked to return in another two weeks when the technician who was away in India would be back.

So Isaac visited the shop a fourth time, only to be given another appointment, three weeks away. Perturbed, Isaac threatened to involve the police. At this point, the shop owner reminded Isaac that he did not have a written guarantee and should therefore pay $50 for repairs. Just then, an attendant pulled Isaac aside and advised him to take the laptop to another retailer where $25 would cover repair costs. With nowhere to turn, a thoroughly disillusioned Isaac ended up having to leave, with no idea of where or how he would raise the $25 he needed to cover repairs on his brand new laptop.

Selling faulty merchandise and pretending to want to do something about it are not the way business should be conducted. The electronics retailer who only offered a verbal guarantee should have immediately replaced Isaac's faulty computer upon presentation of a receipt, no questions asked.

## Compensate for shoddy work

When Judy returned home the day after her house had been fumigated, in spite of the overwhelmingly strong chemical smell in the air, the vermin that should have been exterminated the day before were still alive and highly visible. Judy contacted David, a director with the company that had performed the task and let him know that his team had done a shoddy job. An apologetic David thanked Judy for the information and offered her a complimentary fumigation at the time of her choosing. With so many things going on, Judy did not get around to setting an appointment for the complimentary fumigation until ten months later. When she finally made the call, David was grateful for the opportunity Judy was giving his company to make up for their mistake. David also remembered that the job was to be complimentary. A team was dispatched to Judy's house and this time, even perfectionist Judy admitted that the team did an excellent job.

Admittedly, the team should have got it right the first time, but David earns kudos for acknowledging the team's poor job and offering a complimentary replacement which far exceeded Judy's expectations.

## Actions speak louder than words

When I discovered a new fashion studio that specialized in western style clothes sewn from African prints I was incredibly pleased with myself for finally finding a place with tailors who actually use the measurements they take. At least the first time I ordered a dress there, they did. When I ordered a second outfit, each time I went back for a fitting, something else had gone wrong. If the neckline was too deep today, at the next fitting the neckline was fine but the dress was far too loose. This happened at least seven times, over a period of five months. Thankfully, the studio relocated to a mall close to my office about halfway through my ordeal, a much more convenient location for my numerous fittings. Interestingly enough, each time I was at the studio for another fitting, I dealt with a different tailor. No wonder the results were never what I expected.

Finally, after the seventh unsuccessful fitting for the same dress, I simply lost interest and respectfully requested a refund. To my utter delight, the apologetic Davine secured me a complete refund. The icing on the cake however was management's decision to offer me a replacement dress free of charge, with the guarantee of a better experience, backed by their new team of reliable tailors. The corrective actions taken clearly demonstrated the value the fashion studio attached to retaining this customer. How do you compensate customers when things do not go the way they expected them to?

## Compensate even when another employee did it

Although Jackie and I were laughing as we teased our waiter over his apparent reluctance to let the chef know we had been served cold food, we were far from amused. Fortunately, just then Louie stopped at our table and introduced himself as a corporate sales manager. He wanted to know if we were enjoying our evening.

The cold vegetable samosas (triangular stuffed pastries) were still on our table so, I narrated our story. Louie apologized, offered to notify the chef and personally cleared our table of the chipped chinaware our snack had been served on. No sooner had Louie left than David the chef came by, apologized in person and offered us complimentary replacement servings. The replacement servings were piping hot, with the only downside being that they were all beef samosas, not vegetable ones. Given the team effort made to rectify the situation however, Jackie and I opted to ignore that oversight and dwell on the positive. We then went on to enjoy the rest of the evening under Louie's very watchful eye. He constantly checked to see if everything was exactly the way we wanted it to be.

Do you take immediate corrective action for mistakes, even those made by another member of staff? As a result of Louie and David's efforts, Jackie and I will definitely give that restaurant another try in the very near future.

It is almost like the cold samosa mishap at the beginning of our evening did not even happen. Do your wronged customers leave in a positive frame of mind?

## Points to Ponder

1. How have your front line team mates been instructed to handle customer complaints?

2. How do you really feel about those receipts that say "Goods once sold cannot be returned?" Does your company issue receipts with those words on them and when are you going to get rid of them?

3. What is your reaction when a customer complains about your services or products not meeting their standards e.g. when you serve cold food or lukewarm tea or when the radio they purchased from you stops working after three days?

4. How do you compensate unhappy customers? Does your company have a position on this?

5. Does your company track customer complaints? If yes, what do you about them? How do you make sure that you use feedback from unhappy customers to improve

6. If you do not track unhappy customer feedback, why not and when are you going to begin?

## To Do List

- Invite your team to brainstorm on the different areas where your company might not measure up to customer expectations.

- For each item on the list, ask the team to:
    (a) Find a way to eliminate poor performance
    (b) Design an easy way for customers to make their opinion known and receive compensation
    (c) Define the compensation to be offered.

## How Are You Doing?

If a principle is one that you currently practice, put a tick (√) in the Yes column. If a principle is one you need to work on, put a tick in the No column.

| **Compensate For Errors** | Yes | No |
|---|---|---|
| Apologize for mistakes | | |
| Demonstrate your apology | | |
| Admit and correct mistakes | | |
| Offer helpful responses | | |
| Correct errors promptly | | |
| Repair or replace faulty products | | |
| Compensate for shoddy work | | |
| Actions speak louder than words | | |
| Compensate even when another employee did it | | |

# CHAPTER 12
## Demonstrate Appreciation

Do you know of anyone who does not appreciate a well-earned or well-deserved reward? All the people I know enjoy the rewards they receive and available research shows that most people value being shown appreciation for something they have done. In the same way, customers like to be rewarded. For all the time and money customers spend on your products or services, have you ever done anything to show them that you appreciate the choice they made when they chose to come to you? A small token of appreciation will surely draw those customers back to you. This is why companies initiate loyalty programmes – a means of tracking customer purchases and rewarding them once they reach a pre-specified level.

Airlines for example, have frequent flyer programmes where travellers with the highest number of air miles enjoy special privileges like automatic upgrades from economy to business class and priority boarding. Retailers offer a discount once you spend a given amount of money with them, within a period of six months. Coffee shops issue loyalty cards that get stamped each time you buy a cup of coffee. After ten stamps, your eleventh cup of coffee is free. What are you doing to reward your loyal customers and keep them coming back for more?

It appears that not nearly enough service providers are doing anything to demonstrate customer appreciation. Customers hardly ever even hear the word "Thank you," as they leave a place where they have just spent what they consider to be a lot of money! Growing up, I remember my parents insisting that we children should always thank anyone

## DEMONSTRATE APPRECIATION

who either gave us something or did something for us. "Even when the check-out clerk in a shop hands you your change, it's your change, but you still need to say thank you!" That is the attitude of gratitude that I grew up with. Saying thank you is simply good manners. So why will most customers tell you that the businesses they support with their hard earned money never demonstrate appreciation at all?

If I feel appreciated, I will be sure to return. Research data[viii] shows that it will cost you five times more to get a new customer to try one of your new products than it will to get an existing customer to try a new product. The data also shows that on average, an existing customer will spend up to three times more a year than a new customer. It therefore makes sound business sense to not only attract customers, but to also go out of your way to retain them. In addition to offering exemplary service, demonstrate customer appreciation through tangible customer rewards.

Naturally, that means actually giving something to the customer. Give them more of what they came in for. Our fresh fruit and vegetable market vendors are masters of the art of handing out two or three extra units of whatever you purchase from them - extra oranges or extra onions as the case may be. Even though they have never attended a class on customer service, they know instinctively that you will appreciate getting a little more of something you are already interested in, at no cost to you.

Some companies make it their business to hand you products you have absolutely no use for in supposed appreciation of your patronage. Well- knit baby socks, when all your children are in college, that free lipstick in a shade you will never wear or the complimentary scent that smells like the air freshener at your dentist's. Companies in this category want to make you think they are doing something for you when in reality they are using you as a way to get rid of excess inventory or items that were ordered in error.

Another facade is presented by companies like a regional supermarket chain that offers customers a reward card, allowing them to earn points for purchases. When customers attempt to redeem their points however, they are informed that there is no mechanism by which this can be done. As far as I am concerned, that is known as deception. The supermarket chain however, thinks it is a clever way of making customers think they will be getting rewards to spend in the supermarket at some point in the future. There really is no need for such under-handed tactics. Besides, you will soon be found out.

If you are hard-pressed to come up with a complimentary item that your customers will appreciate, give them more of what they already buy from you or, put money back in their pockets by offering them an unexpected and reasonable price discount or, credit towards their next purchase.

Beyond that demonstrate your appreciation by doing everything you can to fulfil customer requests, even the unusual ones and most important of all, demonstrate that they mean something to you by addressing them by name. Then stand back and watch them literally keep coming back!

## Address customers by name

Do you view your customers as individuals or as nameless numbers? At the office, we typically pay our bills well ahead of time, to the chagrin of our accountant who prefers that we hold off on paying bills until the very last possible minute. One month, by sheer oversight, we were off our early bill payment schedule and in the middle of the month, I received a text message from our phone company, addressed to "Dear esteemed customer." The message informed me that my mobile phone bill was due for payment and that my line would be suspended if I did not pay my dues within seven days. I could however "Ignore if paid." A number to call for details was also provided. My guess is that every post-paid customer who had not paid the previous month's bill by the middle of the month received exactly the same nameless general announcement. When you consider that companies outside the telecommunications sector like banks and our local water and sewerage corporation to mention but two, send their customers tailored text messages with specific account information, this nameless text message approach from a phone company leaves much to be desired.

The phone company does not find it important enough to treat loyal, post-paid customers as individuals. Instead, it should emulate the example set by companies in other fields, which effectively use telecommunications to deliver personalized messages that show customers they are more than just numbers.

## Absorb costs where possible

Few people if any fly for the in-flight food service. Nevertheless, it is appreciated. On a four hour flight between two US cities aboard a US carrier, we had been flying for 45 minutes before a flight attendant announced that complimentary snacks and non-alcoholic beverages would be served to economy passengers. Any economy passenger looking for something more substantial like a sandwich; would have to part with US$5 – 8 for that privilege and US$5 – 7 for an alcoholic beverage. Passengers could choose one of three snacks -two packets of peanuts (about ten peanuts per packet), 1 packet of mini hard pretzels (about five pretzels per packet) or two cookies. Thinking the light snack was a precursor to the ensuing lunch, I eagerly awaited the meal service. An hour later, an attendant walked down the aisle again, with lo and behold, exactly the same snacks as before. Chuckling to myself, I wondered why the airline had even bothered with that second service.

Our African airlines may leave a lot to be desired but at least for now, airline ticket fees still cover a complimentary and much more substantial snack, even on the short 45 minute jaunt between Entebbe and Nairobi. In spite of the challenging times facing the industry, must the airlines really pass every possible cost on to their passengers? Find creative ways to absorb costs so that your customers are not made to feel like you are squeezing every last penny out of their pockets.

## Accommodate loyal customers' requests

I was at a Korean restaurant that I used to frequent, to place an order for take-away food. After placing my order, my waiter asked me for my ten percent discount card which I did not have with me. In the past when this happened, the supervisor on duty simply looked up my card number in the restaurant's records, and went ahead to issue my ten percent discount. On this occasion however, the supervisor on duty adamantly refused to look up my number and consequently, refused to give me the discount. She informed me that "The book lost" and "System no let me." When invoking my frequent customer status failed, I threatened to boycott the restaurant and never to recommend it to anyone again. The supervisor's response: "You free."

My decision never to darken that restaurant's door again was swift and final. Not because I did not receive the negligible ten percent discount. Rather, it was because of the supervisor's rude, rigid and inflexible attitude. She knew me to be a loyal customer but attached no value to that whatsoever. Instead of doing everything possible to satisfy this customer, the supervisor chose to aggravate me; effectively pushing me to visit some of Kampala's numerous new restaurants to find a replacement. Go out of your way to accommodate requests made by loyal customers. It is one way of showing you appreciate their patronage.

## Value all customers

Does your company value all customers, irrespective of their monetary value? My friend Godfrey closed one of his Kampala based businesses and no longer needed the web hosting services of a US-based provider. When the web hosting annual subscription date rolled around, Godfrey simply opted not to renew. Imagine his surprise the next morning, when he received an e-mail from the US-based company's CEO, thanking his company for its patronage and wondering if there was anything the company could do to keep Godfrey's company as a client. Godfrey says the e-mail felt so personal that he replied immediately; explaining that he was pleased with the services but unfortunately his company had closed, eliminating the need for web hosting. Godfrey promised to refer everyone he knows to that company should any of them ask him for a web hosting recommendation. Now, one could say that the e-mail was probably an automatically generated communication that is sent to every client who opts out of a subscription. Even if that were true, it does not change the fact that the e-mail left Godfrey feeling incredibly important. Was Godfrey's company a high value account? Just US$ 94 annually!

His US provider made Godfrey feel truly valued in spite of his distant location and the seemingly low value of his account. When he eventually does need web hosting again, you know he will be getting back in touch with that company. Can all your customers say they feel truly valued by your business?

## Surprise your customers

How do you feel about receiving pleasant surprises? More often than not, when our administrative assistant returns to the office after a round of delivering cheques, she has a horror story or two to tell about one thing or another. Following one such trip however, she returned to the office wearing a wide grin. "You won't believe the surprise from our internet service provider!" she exclaimed. My cynical response: "Shock me – tell me they lowered our rates!" "Actually they did!" came the excited reply. I was pleasantly surprised to learn that our internet service provider had indeed lowered their monthly internet charges by an incredibly large 61 percent! While I know we have the competition to thank for our provider's apparent generosity and the cynic in me thinks it is about time the service providers in our telecommunications industry stopped enjoying abnormal profits, I was still incredibly pleased by the development. I only hoped it was a permanent rate reduction and not just a temporary discount.

Literally putting money back in your customers' pockets is always well received. Not every company can do that but how else might your company demonstrate customer appreciation? Consider offering something complimentary that is related to the services you provide.

## Treat loyal customers like royalty

How do you make loyal customers feel special? Cynthia goes to Johannesburg regularly and stays at the same hotel near the airport. The hotel offers a courtesy airport shuttle, free internet access and discounted corporate rates. For her loyalty, Cynthia always gets the same room, and a special welcome package. On this particular trip, Cynthia's itinerary changed abruptly, putting her in Johannesburg a day earlier than planned. To her delight, Lydia, the hotel's front office duty manager was able to check her into her usual room, even though she was a day early. When Cynthia got to her room, she attributed the absence of her usual welcome treats to her early arrival. As she settled in, an apologetic Inviolatta from Housekeeping showed up with a smile as well as the usual pair of slippers, bottled water, special toiletries and fruit platter. The platter came with a handwritten welcome note from Lydia, the front office manager who had checked her in. Cynthia felt so incredibly special! Cynthia says she will always stay at the same hotel when in Johannesburg because while there, she can depend on receiving royal treatment. It is incredibly important to make your loyal customers feel treasured. Individually, they are your largest source of revenue.

## Appreciate with rewards

Do you reward loyal customers? One could consider the telecommunication price wars to be a roundabout way of rewarding customers. My issue with the price wars however, is that post-paid customers, who I believe are the most loyal and of the highest monetary value, do not get to enjoy the lower promotional rates. Recently, I noticed that one telecommunications company was running a "shs3 per second" promotion that covered both pre and post-paid customers. Congratulations to them for appreciating the latter enough to include them in a promotion! That promotion reminded me of a conversation I had several months ago with a customer service manager at a second telecommunications company (my provider) where I asked if that company would ever reward post-paid customers for their loyalty.

The manager assured me that something was in the pipeline. This week, I received one of those nameless text messages informing me that effective November 1st, post-paid customers would finally get to pay lower rates than the advertised promotional rates. At long last, as a post-paid customer I would get to enjoy a benefit beyond the convenience of not having to load airtime.

It pays to reward your loyal customers for their loyalty. Find a way to make them feel special after all, they are customers you can rely on and when considered individually, each is one of your highest sources of revenue.

# DEMONSTRATE APPRECIATION

*Demonstrate appreciation*

## Offer tangible appreciation

Maggie has been a loyal customer of a US leader in telecommunication services, for several years. That company was therefore Maggie's natural choice when she needed to purchase a PC card that would give her internet access while on a three week trip to a remote location with no Wi-Fi networks. When Maggie called with her order, once the customer service representative confirmed Maggie's identity and thanked her for her loyalty, she repeatedly referred to Maggie by name throughout the ensuing conversation.

Having indicated that she only needed the service for three weeks, Maggie learned that the company offered a 30 day trial period during which she could cancel the service at any time. Maggie would also receive a 100 percent mail-in rebate which if returned to the company would earn her a full refund of the purchase price ($100) of her new PC card. Finally at Maggie's request, to thank her for her loyalty, the representative waived the $30 service activation fee. Having obtained a total of $130 worth of complimentary goods and services, why would Maggie want to go anywhere else? Find ways to tangibly demonstrate customer appreciation and keep loyal customers coming back for more.

## Points to Ponder

1. What does your company do to retain customers?

2. Think back to a time when a company where you are a customer showed you some form of appreciation. What did the company do and how did the gesture make you feel?

3. When did your company last demonstrate appreciation to your customers? What form did the appreciation take and which customers benefitted?

4. Do you know who your most loyal customers are? If not, how will you find out?

5. How do your most loyal customers know they mean something special to your company?

6. Now that you know it is important to demonstrate customer appreciation, what are you going to do about it?

## To Do List

- Invite your team to brainstorm on the different things your company can do to demonstrate customer appreciation. Clearly define the qualifying criteria for each mode of appreciation.

- Create a customer appreciation calendar, showing exactly what will be done for which customers, when and by whom. How much will the activities cost? Make this an annual exercise, not just a one-time activity.

## How Are You Doing?

If a principle is one that you currently practice, put a tick (√) in the Yes column. If a principle is one you need to work on, put a tick in the No column.

| **Demonstrate Appreciation** | Yes | No |
|---|---|---|
| Address customers by name | | |
| Absorb costs where possible | | |
| Accommodate loyal customers' requests | | |
| Value all customers | | |
| Surprise your customers | | |
| Treat loyal customers like royalty | | |
| Appreciate with rewards | | |
| Offer tangible appreciation | | |

## CHAPTER 13
# Equip And Reward Your Staff

C learly, you will not be able to keep your customers coming back for more without the support of your staff. Because they are not magicians and cannot pull different ways of delighting your customers out of thin air, you will need to provide support. Recruit the kind of employees that you feel will support your vision for your business and then equip them with the right tools. Train them on every relevant aspect of your business so that they will be able to answer customer questions knowledgeably. Train them on exactly how you would like to have them treat your customers and even send in "mystery shoppers" who will give you a detailed report on how your staff treated them. In addition to training, give your employees the degree of freedom they will need in order to make quick decisions in the customer's favour, without having to look for you or a supervisor. This will give your employees unprecedented opportunities to demonstrate initiative. Additionally, more autonomy will increase their level of job satisfaction and certainly improve their job performance.

In a part of the world where it is not uncommon for the waiters and waitresses in a restaurant to be prohibited from eating the meals on the premises, is it any wonder that the wait-staff in such a restaurant are unhappy? The wait-staff in these kinds of places typically wear oversize, worn out uniforms and walk to and from work because their meagre salary forces them to choose between eating a meal that night or using public transport and sleeping on an empty stomach. Can you really blame a person in that kind of a situation for being surly when dealing with customers?

Employers who do not view their employees as their most valuable internal asset are making a grave mistake. Valuable assets should be treasured. If they are poorly treated and end up with a negative attitude, they will have a negative impact on your business through their behaviour. Bitterly unhappy employees, sometimes called 'toxic,' will wear their depressing and negative attitude on their faces. Their attitude will not only send away your customers, but it will also rub off on your other employees.

Finally, an unhappy employee will always be on the lookout for the proverbial greener pastures and will leave just as soon as an opportunity presents itself. Although by that time, you might actually be relieved that the individual has left, think of all the resources you invested in them and the business lost on account of their attitude. It is much cheaper to pre-empt the situation by treating employees like the valuable resources that they are, from the beginning. Assuming you made the right hiring decisions, train your staff, give them the freedom to do their job well and appreciate their endeavours to keep you in business by delighting your customers and finally, reward them.

In his US national bestseller *The Starbucks Experience*, Joseph A. Michelli refers to the Starbucks "Green Apron" book[ix]. The book explains to every Starbucks partner what it takes to create the Starbucks Experience for everyone who interacts with the company in any way - be welcoming, be genuine, be considerate, be knowledgeable and be involved. So every partner has a handbook to refer to whenever in doubt about how to deliver the Starbucks Experience. Undergirding the principals in the book is the belief that "Everything Matters." In delivering a delightful customer experience, Starbucks partners and employees all know that nothing is too insignificant to be ignored and they have the freedom to ensure that customers always have memorable experiences with them. Beyond generic training, do your team members have a company-specific set of documented guidelines to provide them with direction and the freedom to follow through? Are there any employees on your staff that have not undergone the training they need to be effective? If not, why not and what are you going to do about it? Training may be in-house, on the job, or at a training facility.

In addition, how do you reward the employees who follow through on what you ask them to do and actually treat your customers the way you would like them to be treated? When you find out that your employees are doing an excellent job of keeping your customers coming back, go beyond the words "thank you" and tangibly demonstrate your appreciation for all they do to keep your business running. If they know their actions are appreciated, they will repeat the behaviour. There are as many ways to demonstrate appreciation as there are people out there. Recognition at the monthly team meetings, their photograph on the wall in the company lobby, privileged parking, gift certificates, a congratulatory team lunch or a weekend out of town with all expenses paid are a few examples of the ways you can reward your employees. You will need to find out what your employees will appreciate, as well as what your business can afford to give.

## Empower employees to make decisions

How much freedom do you allow your staff in making low impact financial decisions? While at one of Kampala's large hotels, I decided to use the opportunity to get passport photographs taken at the in-house photo studio, in the hotel's shopping arcade. Betty the receptionist/cashier and Roger the photographer were both highly customer oriented, cracking jokes with almost everyone who walked in. When my order was ready, Betty discovered that she had inadvertently printed an additional twelve passport photographs for me – perhaps all the jokes had distracted her! Betty asked me to pay for the extra photographs. My position however was that since I had not ordered them she could destroy the pictures and get absolutely nothing for them or, she could take what I was willing to offer for her mistake, US$1.00, and even that, only because I knew I would definitely use the photographs if I took them. Within a few seconds, Betty accepted my offer and I happily left with enough passport photographs for the next five years.

The upbeat employees in the photo studio were empowered to make simple, low-impact financial decisions on the spot. Have you considered giving your employees some degrees of freedom to please a customer?

# EQUIP AND REWARD YOUR STAFF

## Empower employees to resolve issues

Tired of hearing my dry cleaning complaints, my friends suggested I try the dry cleaning service at one of the hotels in town, and so I did. I was immediately impressed by Felly's cheerful greeting and the 24 hour turnaround time. The next day when I went to pick up my suit, there was an area on one of the sleeves that I was not happy about. I expressed this to Felly. Her immediate and simple response was - as long as a customer was not satisfied with any aspect of their work whatsoever, it would be re-done, at no extra charge.

Helen, our office assistant, experienced similar treatment when she returned an unused notebook that was falling apart at the seams, to a stationery shop. When she showed the book to the shop attendant, he immediately recognized it as one of their own, apologized, took the book back and replaced it with a brand new one. Empower your employees to effectively handle complaints on the spot without any hassle.

## Monitor service consistently

How do you know when the quality of your services declines? I happen to be a fan of a small neighbourhood cafe close to my office. I find the food delicious, the prices reasonable and the ambience relaxing. I used to like the service too, until things began to change. The change was so apparent that on one visit to the cafe, I had to ask my waitress if they were under new management. What struck me the most was the attitude of the waiters and waitresses, who simply seemed reluctant to serve their waiting customers. I watched them drag their feet to customer tables, wear glum expressions as they mumbled what they hoped to pass off as a greeting, eventually serve the ordered meal with the same glum expressions and like in so many other places, make customers wait long after their meal was over before bringing the bill. Things had been different as recently as two months prior to that but nobody on the inside seemed to have noticed.

The noticeable yet unaddressed service decline caused me to lower my frequency of visits, stop leaving tips and even stop recommending the cafe to my friends. Every business should have a person to monitor quality standards. This could be done by a member of staff or by an external and objective party.

## Give employees freedom

We all know that nothing commercial is ever really "free of charge" but items that are relevant and seemingly complimentary are typically well received. Armed with a brand new fish recipe book, I was eager to buy some fish and begin experimenting. As soon as my US itinerary allowed me to, I visited a local grocery store and headed straight for the Meat Counter. Tony, the associate, asked me how my day was going, what I was looking for and how many people I would be cooking for. After telling me how much tilapia I needed to buy, Tony dictated his favourite tilapia recipe while I took notes. As if all that was not enough, Tony then gave me the equivalent of 1/4 kilogramme of complimentary tilapia, provided I promised to try his recipe.

That final gesture brought a smile to my face and reminded me of the "jaribu" (sample) or "nyongeza" (bonus) that some of our own market vendors use to attract customers or to give customers a sound reason to return.

Have you developed an appreciation for the attraction of relevant complimentary offers to your customers?

## Reward excellent customer service

Does your company reward excellent customer service? In the past, with neither a national carrier nor a national frequent flyer programme, many Ugandan frequent flyers joined what I will call "foreign" frequent flyer programmes e.g. Flying Blue, Voyager etc. in order to earn rewards for flying. I happen to belong to one of those "foreign" programmes and happily enjoy all the accompanying benefits. Recently, I received an appreciation letter from my favourite carrier, thanking me for my loyalty.

Interestingly enough, in addition to several coupons for a variety of free services, the envelope also included three Recognition Certificates that the airline invited me to issue to any three airline employees that I felt deserved special recognition. Each employee who receives a recognition certificate enters the certificate and its accompanying award code on an employee website where accumulated recognition points are used to redeem a variety of rewards. With attractive and internally visible rewards for excellent service, it is no wonder that employees strive to offer customers pleasant experiences.

Visibly rewarding employees who offer excellent customer service and getting the customers who receive excellent service to participate in the recognition process is one way of motivating your staff to treat your customers the right way. What are you doing to motivate your staff to treat customers the way you want them to?

## Motivate employees with perks

What on-the-job perks do your employees enjoy? It had been two years since my last eye exam so, on a US trip I walked into an optical shop where customers can get an eye exam and have their prescription lenses made and fitted into their selected frame all under one roof. As I waited for the optometrist, an attendant offered to help me choose new frames.

We found the "perfect frame" almost immediately but spent another 20 minutes looking at other options, just to be sure. During our conversation I commented about the price of some of the designer frames, provoking Jason into asking whether my health insurance would cover my expenses.

When I informed him I would be paying cash, Jason immediately offered me his employee discount – 50 percent off my entire purchase! I walked into the optometrist's office convinced Jason was joking. 30 minutes later, new prescription in hand and expecting Jason to have conveniently disappeared, I was pleasantly surprised when he approached me with "our" frames and escorted me to the cashier who prepared my bill and keyed in Jason's 50 percent employee discount. I know this hardly ever happens but even if I never get another discount from that optical chain, it will always be my first US stop for eye care.

It seemed to me, that Jason felt good enough about the perks he enjoyed to want to pass them on. In a conspiratorial whisper, he told me that he was not in the habit of giving out his employee discount. I however, was incredibly pleased that he chose to give it to me. What perks do your employees enjoy? If you are a hotelier, does your staff actually eat hotel meals or as is the case in some hotels, do staff have to look for meals elsewhere? Just by letting your staff enjoy meals on the premises, you will notice an improvement in their level of service provision.

# KEEPING CUSTOMERS

*Reward staff*

## Points to Ponder

1. How much time are you willing to spend on coaching your staff every week?

2. What complimentary services do your employees have the freedom to provide to customers?

3. What kind of decisions can your employees make on their own, without having to get a manager's permission?

4. When was the last time you gave your employees feedback on their performance?

5. What kind of discounted services or products from your business are you able to provide to your employees as a perk for working for you?

6. What does your company do to evaluate employee satisfaction?

## To Do List

- For each product or service you provide, ask you team to create 'the customer's path' described in Chapter One. What steps does a customer go through in order to obtain your product or service? At each step what are the possible sources of pain or pleasure? How will your team eliminate actual or potential pain and enhance the pleasure each customer experiences at each point? Make this an engaging exercise by putting an illustration of 'the customer's path' on the wall.

- List and announce the complimentary products or series that your employees are free to give to customers. Provide clear guidelines so that everyone is clear on customer actions that trigger offers, the number of offers employees are allowed to make and the maximum value of offers within a given period of time, for example one or six months.

- Ask your team to help you create a monthly customer service recognition award. Let the team determine the winner selection criteria as well as the reward.

- Appoint a customer service champion whose role will be to see to it that excellent customer service (by the customer's definition, not the company's) becomes a company reality.

## How Are You Doing?

If a principle is one that you currently practice, put a tick (√) in the Yes column. If a principle is one you need to work on, put a tick in the No column.

| Equip and Reward Your Staff | Yes | No |
|---|---|---|
| Empower employees to make decisions | | |
| Accommodate reasonable requests | | |
| Empower employees to resolve issues | | |
| Monitor service consistently | | |
| Reward excellent customer service | | |
| Motivate employees with perks | | |

# CHAPTER 14
## MONITOR THE COMPETITION

No matter how good you think you are at what you do, it is important to keep an eye on the competition. If the competition's doors are open, surely they are doing something right. What is it that makes customers spend their money on the competition instead of on you? What makes customers bypass the competition and come to you? Know what sets you apart and know what your competition stands for.

The best way for you to find out why customers flock to your door is to ask them. One of the best ways for you to find out why customers flock to your competition is to actually visit the competition and find out what they are doing right. While you are at it, it would not be a bad idea to find out what they are doing wrong – one more thing for you to make sure you avoid doing. You or a member of your team should pay the competition a visit on a regular basis. This is easier to do with some businesses than with others but, on the whole, you should be able to find an efficient and informative way of monitoring what your competition is up to. Some retailers let customers know that they will beat any competitor's price. Shoppers looking for a bargain therefore become a reliable source of information on competitor prices.

Visit your competitor's website if they have one, to find out more about your competition. Become your competition's customer. If you are an hotelier, it will not hurt you to spend a night in your competition's hotel or even order a meal there. Walk into your competitor's supermarket, walk around, look around, ask an attendant for help and yes, go

## MONITOR THE COMPETITION

ahead and actually buy something. The experience will reveal a wealth of information. Call the competition's number and see how they handle telephone calls. Send an e-mail to your competitor's e-mail address and see how they respond, if at all. All this will give you valuable information on how the competition handles customers, compared to you. Do your best to be objective in your analysis, giving your competition credit where it is due.

Who exactly is your competition? Literally speaking, that would be every business that offers the same product or service that you offer, depending of course on how you define what you offer. One could say that Shell and Mogas are competitors. Shell could argue however, that by offering a much wider range of products and a much higher number of well distributed, well located service stations, they far outdistance Mogas and would not even consider them to be one of their competitors. They simply do not offer the same thing.

Another school of thought takes an even broader brush and considers the competition to be anything that competes for expenditure for instance, soft drink companies talk about "share of stomach" and any company that competes for a consumer's share of stomach is considered the competition. Taking such a broad view of their categories allowed soft drink manufacturers to expand into fruit juices and even water.

What is your offer, who is your customer and who is your competition? Just like it is important for you to walk in your customer's shoes in order to find out exactly what customers go through when they interact with you, your product or service; it is important for you to experience what your competitors' customers experience too. It will be good for you. Go ahead and try it.

# KEEPING CUSTOMERS

*Check on the competition*

## Points to Ponder

1. How often do you personally take stock of what your competition is doing?

2. How different are your products or services from your competition?

3. How different is your offer from your competition's offer?

4. Why should customers come to you and not to your competition?

5. Why do customers go to your competition instead of coming to you?

6. How will you stay ahead of your competition?

## To Do List

- Ask team members to volunteer to visit the competition and actually purchase a product or service. This should be a regular activity. Identify the three main differences between your offer and your competition's.

- Ask your most loyal customers what they think about what the competition has to offer and find out why your most loyal customers remain with you.

## How Are You Doing?

If a principle is one that you currently practice, put a tick (√) in the Yes column. If a principle is one you need to work on, put a tick in the No column.

| Monitor the Competition | Yes | No |
|---|---|---|
| Ask customers about the competition | | |
| Visit the competition's website | | |
| Visit the competition | | |
| Try the competition's product | | |
| Identify the competition's strengths | | |
| Identify the competition's weaknesses | | |

# CHAPTER 15
## PUT IT INTO PRACTICE

If you are reading this chapter after going through the entire book – some readers like to start books at the end – then you have literally walked through the different stages a customer may go through in conducting business with you. As you read the real life cases in each chapter, I hope you were able to put yourself in both the service provider's and the customer's shoes. As a customer, how should you have been treated? As a service provider would you have followed the same path as was followed and if not, what would you have done differently? What will you do differently going forward, now that you have a slightly different lens to look through? If you are a student of customer service, this book should have helped you walk a mile in your customers' shoes. How comfortable were they and how will you make sure your customers' shoes always fit them comfortably, at least when they are transacting business with you or receiving service from you?

Business owners, managers, supervisors, team leaders, government ministers – whatever your title – if you are in a leadership position, always remember that there is a whole crowd looking to you for cues on how to behave. If you do not embrace delighting customers as the way to do things, nobody else will.

For the sake of your business, never forget that without your customers, you would be out of business. Customers have a need that your business is able to fulfil, therefore your business exists. Without them, your business would close its doors. So treat customers like the extraordinarily important individuals they are. Address them by name, establish

# PUT IT INTO PRACTICE

and nurture a relationship with them. Delight them and they will be back time and time again, bringing friends and family in tow.

Remember to take action. Use this book as a reference tool, to coach your employees, at your team meetings and in your training sessions. Turn responses to the "Points to Ponder" into actual projects. Go ahead and implement the assignments in the "To Do List" as soon as tomorrow. That is exactly what they are for.

Finally, e-mail me your comments, questions and updates on how you are doing. I am eager to hear about the changes you have made and the impact those changes have had on you as an individual and on your business.

To simply get in touch or to book a "Keeping Customers" workshop, e-mail me at:

**keepingcustomers@dmtconsultants.net**

# END NOTES

**Chapter One**

i. *Business Management System,* The International Trade Centre, Geneva.

ii. *Leading on the Edge of Chaos,* Emmett C. Murphy and Mark A. Murphy, Prentice Hall Press, March 2002.

iii. *Customer Relationships are Key to Your Marketing Strategy,* Laura Lake, About.com Guide.

iv. *Business Management System,* The International Trade Centre, Geneva.

**Chapter Three**

v. *The Power of Nice,* Linda Kaplan Thaler and Robin Kawal, DoubleDay 2006, pg. 11.

vi. *Be Our Guest,* The Disney Institute, Disney Editions, NY, 2001, pg. 58.

**Chapter Eleven**

vii. Businesscoach.com

**Chapter Twelve**

viii. *Repeat Customers Spend 33% More Than New Customers,* www.retailactive.com/, November 2008

**Chapter Thirteen**

ix. *The Starbucks Experience,* Joseph A. Michelli, McGraw Hill, 2007, pg. 21.

www.ingramcontent.com/pod-product-compliance
Lightning Source LLC
Chambersburg PA
CBHW020644220526
45464CB00001B/290